15 Aug. 05

To Ellen,

May Love Always
Warm Your Heart.

Walking on the Grass

Walking on the Grass

CARLA MANCARI

on the Grass

A WHITE WOMAN
IN A BLACK WORLD

MERCER UNIVERSITY PRESS 2001

ISBN 0-86554-717-3
MUP/H537

First Edition.

∞The paper used in this publication meets the minimum requirements of
American National Standard for Information Sciences—Permanence of
Paper for Printed Library Materials, ANSI Z39.48-1992.

Library of Congress Cataloging-in-Publication Data

Mancari, C. R. (Carla R.), 1933-
Walking on the grass : a white woman in a black world / C.R.
Mancari.—1st ed.
    p. cm.
Includes bibliographical references and index.
ISBN 0-86554-717-3 (hardcover : alk. paper)
1. Mancari, C. R. (Carla R.), 1933- 2. White women—United States—
Biography. 3. College students—South Carolina—Orangeburg—
Biography. 4. South Carolina State College—Biography. 5. Orangeburg
(S.C.)—Race relations. 6. African American universities and colleges—
South Carolina—Orangeburg. 7. Racism—United States—Case studies.
I. Title.
E185.98.M36 A3 2001
378.757'79—dc21

                                                            2001005889

Dedicated to the Recognition and Memory

of

Delano Middleton

Samuel Hammond Jr.

Henry Smith

Contents

Acknowledgments

This story was a joint effort. Many individuals made the experiences possible.

My continuous love to my parents, Elizabeth and Frank Mancari, who always loved and nourished me, a less than perfect child.

A heartfelt thanks to my friend Mary T, who helped set my sights in the direction of a higher education. Her care and support was the fuel that propelled me on.

There were three college deans in my life without which this story would not have been lived much less written.

Dean Sister Mary Albert, Our Lady of Mercy Junior College, Charleston, South Carolina, was the first to say "yes, you may try," when the test scores said no. Without her, the outer journey would not have taken place and the inner one would never have begun.

Dean H. Frank Trotter, University of South Carolina, who said "yes" when the test scores were so low that I had been turned down by the university administrators. He gave me the opportunity to try, and in addition he gave me a tool for all of my counseling years when he said, "Carla, no one can sit across from another individual and measure the motivational drive that exists within the individual—that cannot be tested."

Dean Brooks, South Carolina State College, the warm, and caring dean who told the president of the college, "I want to allow her to attend." He accepted a white person on face value and helped her to attain much more than she had bargained for.

A special thanks to the professors and students at South Carolina State College who allowed me to share for a time their world. They made a transformation possible.

My appreciation to Wesley Smith, who encouraged me to write the story.

My thanks to Deana Holloway who searched out a reel-to-reel tape recorder and helped transcribe the original taped diary.

To Margaret Renee Head who reviewed and edited the first draft, a big thank you.

I am eternally indebted to Henry T. Snelling, who gave his generous time and effort without reward. He patiently edited and guided the manuscript to its final form. In him, the manuscript, and the author, found a friend.

I am blessed with the love and constant support of a large family, especially two sisters, Mary Bensinger and Dolly Mancari. They are always there when I need them. It is a family thing that I am fortunate to have.

To the creator of us all, I marvel at the guidance attended and the mind, heart, and soul experience allowed.

In addition, of course, my gratitude for Joshua whose patience and antics helped maintain the proper perspective as I relived the entire journey.

Introduction

In the space of a single year, Carla accomplished more than some people do in an entire lifetime.

Though she did not have a high school diploma, she enrolled in a graduate school and earned a master's degree.

Although she successfully overcame the deficiencies in her academic credentials, she managed to turn virtually the entire student body of her graduate school against her, simply because her skin was the wrong color.

While attending class her life was placed at risk when deadly riots—some involving her classmates—broke out on and around the campus. Tragically, some of her fellow students were among the victims.

In the process of obtaining her graduate degree, she also managed to alienate virtually all the people she had known and worked with, including the supervisor on her job, who made it clear that she was a pariah. She was soon out of a job.

Within that same short year, she found and married the man of her dreams, only to discover that he marched to a tune of a different moral drummer. Their differences on the issue of race would quickly threaten their marriage.

And a medical emergency threatened her very existence. It was a year packed with every emotion a human could experience, from deep love to brutal hatred, from unabashed joy to paralyzing fear.

It was the worst year of her life. And the best. This is her story of the events of that year.

1

The Lights Go Out

A warm drizzle affectionately grazed Carla's dark lashes as she left the dorm. As she retrieved a raincoat from her car, the campus seemed quaint. The smallness of the college wrapped its quaintness in a southern charm complimented by narrow walks, pathways, and grassy slopes.

The radiant, scented azaleas for which this area of South Carolina was well known were long past their prime. What remained were large green shrubs near the campus buildings and the many lovely rose bushes stalked by huge oak trees.

It was a pleasant day in the middle of June 1967. The campus atmosphere was one of reserved, quiet-calm. A calm that clouded her mind from the encroaching reality. Her first impression, "I think I am going to like it here." Her first stop was the gym. Carla strode out confidently. It was well that she was not overly cautious, for the journey had begun. Crossing the main avenue that led to the rear entrance of the gym building, she climbed a wide set of stairs and walked up to a partly opened door. At the entrance was a tall solitary black male. He saw her and almost smiled, but not quite. Nervously, Carla nodded and walked quickly past him. Unlike the subdued rainy campus, the gym was bustling with activity.

Registration was reminiscent of Carla's undergraduate days at the University of South Carolina: long tables with individuals attending them, students standing in line, and happy talk of friends reunited after weeks apart during semester break filled the room.

Of course, there was one monumental difference this time: save one, every face in the room was black.

The warm drizzle left behind moments before became a downpour of cold stares. All eyes and heads turned in Carla's direction. Momentarily, she was disoriented and frozen in her tracks as her heart skipped a beat on its way to her throat. Her throat constricted, her lips quivered and her mouth dried, it was difficult to swallow.

Immersed in a sea of black, Carla felt she had skirted the edges of the universe and discordant thoughts rose to torment her. She had never seen so many black faces in one place. Her diverging emotions could not be organized. Everything seemed wrong, white was nowhere to be found.

Faced with a distorted shadowed reflection of her world, she struggled to restore her equilibrium. This time, she was the minority. She was different because of the color of her skin. The enormity of this hit her as if the lights had gone out all over the world.

Those around her temporarily lost their balance and conversations stopped in mid-sentence. The students' somber, amazed expressions momentarily flung her into a downward spiral. Their anger preyed upon her like a double-edged sword. Carla's body deflected hostile cuts; the not-so-subtle message in the surprised reaction of the students was clear: "What are you doing here? Go away and leave us alone."

The moment of shock slipped into the past. Equilibrium restored, Carla's pride kicked in. With an exertion of mind, she regained the possession of her thoughts. "I'm not going to give any of you people the satisfaction of acting weak or uncertain. I have a purpose for being here and by golly I'm going to accomplish it." Taking a deep breath, without looking left or right, Carla walked with a determined step past a long line of stone-faced students. She went to a table where there was no line and had her class cards, tuition bills, and meal ticket stamped paid.

"Be sure you don't lose that meal ticket. It has to last nine weeks," cautioned the dark-skinned woman sitting behind the table. Carla nodded but wondered, "Is she taunting me? Does she think I'm stupid?" In Carla's stunned state, she couldn't tell. Retracing her steps in haste, she left.

Next stop was the bookstore in the administration building, but Carla wasn't sure how to get there. It was only two weeks ago that she and a friend had visited the dean there.

Searching her memory, she found the building. Climbing the steps, Carla passed through the doors and a sign instructed her to go down a narrow staircase for the bookstore.

She viewed an area enclosed by a long wooden counter with teller windows on both sides. Long lines of students stood before each window.

For the first time, she was in dread—in dread of having to take a place among "them." No short cut, she had to wait her turn. Hesitantly, Carla walked to the shorter of the two slow-moving lines. She stood quietly and alone. "I may as well be invisible; I wish I were." Within the hour, her optimistic mood was shattered as she fell into utter despair.

Trying to smile, and striving with all possible effort, Carla mustered the courage to attempt a little small talk. No one returned the gesture. The battle was lost. Ignored, she retreated into a remorseful silence and listened to the conversations around her.

"Hi, Millie. Glad you're back. Come over to my dorm room later."

"Mike! My man! Where the hell have you been?"

"Jan, did you get to room with Bertha? This is going to be one tough semester."

Conversation and recognition were only among the others. Standing quietly and invisible for almost two hours, Carla edged slowly to the front. With her head pounding, her legs and feet aching, and her stomach growling with hunger she drew in and tightened her stomach, she hoped that no one heard the thunder of hunger.

A matronly woman greeted her with a curt, "May I help you?" Barely managing, Carla handed her the paper that listed the desired books. Receiving the books, she quickly removed herself from the line. All was accomplished without having said a word.

Heading directly back to the safety and privacy of her dorm room, Carla was emotionally drained. Collapsing upon the bed, she felt she had been ambushed by an obscured reality. Every part of her was hurting, yet rethinking the day's events overshadowed her body's needs.

The road to registration seemed to have taken a thousand turns since meeting with the dean two weeks earlier. The day's events had plunged her into a discontented haze. She had failed in her base attempt at being welcomed and now she was living in a corner under their shadow stumbling in the darkness.

Suffering from the effects of an alarming unexpected registration, she was aware that she found herself in circumstances beyond her control. The very thought of what the next moment might bring terrified her.

But what placed Carla Mancari there in the first place? What force could possibly have caused her to depart from what she considered to be the white "norm" for a world of blackness?

Within each of us there's a warm, safe place. It's a place in a world protected from those who would do us harm. It's a world we can easily slip into whenever we feel threatened by the realities around us. Carla didn't create this world, she discovered it.

Carla's parents were Italian immigrants who settled in Delaware. She was the tenth of their twelve children. She remembers her parents as loving and hardworking.

A sickly baby, she had dark-brown hair and large, oval dark-brown eyes. Carla grew into a fragile child who seemed not to be very bright. Feeling disconnected from the real world, she retreated into an inner world for safekeeping. Far from the noise of this world, she rested in the stillness of her own individual being.

She attended segregated Catholic schools and lived in all-white neighborhoods. Her conditioning by family, teachers, religious leaders and peers implied blacks were inferior, less than human.

The very idea of mixing or associating with blacks in school, neighborhood or social activities was unthinkable. The northern white segregationist beliefs ran parallel with the old south racist teachings. All of the myths and fear of Negroes were imbedded in Carla's consciousness.

Loved at home but ridiculed at school, twice held back, Carla developed a tenacious spirit that challenged authority.

In the fourth grade, Carla challenged the bishop during a sermon before her class, causing him to inquire of the nun, "Who is this child who dared to question me?"

In an almost helpless gesture, Sister replied, "She apparently is in need of religious instruction. She's a very determined child."

A subtle smile could be detected on the old bishop's disciplined lips as he turned in a huff and stormed out of the school, saying, "It will either carry her far, or destroy her early."

Carla's performance in eighth grade was so poor that she didn't go to high school. Instead, she entered a two-year office-training program, a Catholic-run all-girl school.

The ability to grasp the most general of office skills was beyond her range and she continued to fail. Her ability to escape within herself made it possible to tolerate school, but it also kept her from learning.

A week before graduation, the nuns conducted a job clinic. Excluded from this program because of poor grades, Carla found a job on her own. She hastened to the classroom to happily share her good news with the black-and-white-robed nun. Like a gigantic penguin nervously waving its flippers, Sister lurched out of her chair, and in anger shouted, "How dare you take it upon yourself to find a job without my permission?" Pointing to a seat, Sister yelled, "I will deal with you later." The entire class laughed.

Defiantly, Carla walked to the door, "Carla, walk through that door and you will not graduate with your class next week." Turning her head slightly in Sister's direction, Carla's eyes penetrated hers contemptuously. She opened the door, walked out and slammed it behind her.

"To hell with Sister and to hell with school," she muttered aloud.

Carla's mom had a different idea about hell and how to deal with Sister. Through all the years of failure and difficulty, she never complained or faltered in her love for Carla. Now, she finally had something to be proud of—Carla was to graduate from a two-year school program. It was not high school, but it was a graduation nonetheless. For her mom, who couldn't read or write, this was a major accomplishment, one to cherish, not thrown away in a temper tantrum.

In a soft but firm voice came the order, "You will go to the convent, put aside your anger, swallow your pride and apologize."

The night before graduation, Carla was to do the unthinkable, face Sister. It was easier, she thought, if she were asked to ride a tidal wave of the worst magnitude. Carla rang the door bell. A young, soft-spoken nun opened the door, and motioned Carla to step into the foyer. In a little more than a whisper, she asked to see Sister.

The click of heels disrupted the silence. Sister's bellowing cut through the stillness of the convent as she shouted "hardheaded," "willful," "lazy," and "stubborn." Carla gazed down at the cracks in the shiny wood floor beneath her feet, silently wishing they would swallow her. Carla considered her options; there were none.

Satisfied that she was not going to get a retort from Carla, Sister went into the hall closet, reached for a large box from a high shelf, and flung it at Carla. It was her cap and gown. Mumbling a quick "thank you," she wasted no time in making a speedy exit. It was Carla's fondest hope that this was one relationship that had no long term connections.

The next morning, Carla's proud mom sat in church, love in her heart and tears in her eyes, as she watched her misfit daughter walking down the center aisle—the oldest in the class, but a graduate nonetheless. A gift of love to her mom, who finally had something to brag about concerning her tenth child.

She was 18, a grocery chain hired her as a cashier, a job she held for four years. Through those years, Carla didn't associate or socialize with as much as one black employee. The racial confusions that infested her mind allowed Carla's Christian all-white world of racist beliefs to remain intact.

For a while, Carla was satisfied. Until, she was drawn to a discontented unravelling of her mental complacency bondage. Then she wanted more, she wanted out of the dead-end rut to which she had condemned herself.

A gray, dismal, cold day in December found Carla waiting for a bus in front of the downtown post office. Someone, somewhere was watching her. Carla could feel the penetration of strong, demanding eyes. She cautiously turned her head. Her attention was drawn to a large picture of a serious, tight-lipped Uncle Sam pointing and saying, "I want you."

Carla instantly turned, walked inside the post office to the Air Force recruiting office. The deed was done.

Riding the bus home, she was hammered by panic and doubts. "I've never been away from home before. Can I really succeed on my own? How will I ever tell my parents? I don't want to hurt them? God what've I done?"

"Why would you do such a thing?" asked Pop. He was puzzled why she would consider leaving the protection of a loving home.

"The Air Force offers the opportunity for further education." Pangs of remorse began to pervade her conscience.

"Is that what you really want?" Mom softly questioned.

"Yes, it is. Despite her childhood experiences, a drive for a better education rose early in Carla's adult life. The Air Force seemed a devious way of circumventing the impossible.

Pop looked hard with care on his tenth child. "All right, if it's what you want. But honey," he warned, "be careful and stay focused on your intentions. Dreams have a tendency of fading when they're not attended."

Within Carla's inner world of safety, a potent force had nudged her into the outer river of life. She must learn to swim as she was about to experience the eddies and banks along life's way.

Three days later, a lump in her throat and holding back tears, she was on her way. Carla promised herself she wouldn't fail. She would complete basic training and serve the enlisted time.

The Air Force sent Carla to the deep South, far from the site of her childhood failures. Stationed at the Air Force base in Charleston, South Carolina, Carla performed the duties of a purchasing agent. She found the work interesting.

It was here she met a wonderful person who changed her life, Mary Thompson. Everyone affectionately called her Mary T. The first time Carla met Mary T, she noticed her golden-blond hair, which was surprising in a woman in her fifties. But mostly she was aware of Mary T's deep, blue-green eyes, which promised a gentle and loving personality. Never over their long friendship was that promise to be broken. Her advice and friendship helped guided Carla.

In her new friend Carla, Mary T saw a young woman she would have been proud to call her daughter—single, twenty-three years old, slender, petite, and of medium height. Her thick dark brown hair was worn to the sides, allowing it to gently wave to her shoulders. With a smooth, glowing complexion and warm, inviting smile, Mary T considered Carla attractive. Although Carla kept in close contact with her parents, it was good to have the protection of a loving mother-figure far from home.

Mary T instilled in Carla an appreciation of self and self-worth. She reinforced the concept of not allowing anyone to take advantage of her, to stand up for what she believed in. This kind of encouragement was very different from Carla's previous school years. The opportunity to put to the test this new-found idea of self-worth presented itself almost immediately.

Two married male sergeants with whom Carla worked repeatedly made explicit sexual advances. She reported this to the WAF major, who instructed Carla to write down what was happening. After reading the reports, the major did nothing.

Pushed over the edge, Carla's innate drive to challenge authority rose. Outraged by the sergeants' misbehavior and the inaction by the major, Carla, accompanied by Mary T, drove directly to the Pentagon in Washington, D.C.

Without being stopped or questioned, they entered the Pentagon. They located the WAF commander's office, approached the secretary, and requested to see the commander. Stunned by Carla's presence at her desk, the secretary immediately went into the commander's office.

Astonished at an airman second class who dared to approach a WAF commander, she came out immediately, greeted Carla and Mary T. After ushering them into her office, she came straight to the point: "Why are you here?"

"I want to stop the unwanted sexual advances against myself and the other WAF personnel at the base," Carla blurted out.

Shaking her head in wonderment at this young woman who would dare to breach the military chain of command, the commander promised, "All right, I'll keep your visit confidential for your own protection, and I'll look into the working conditions of the women assigned to the base with an unannounced inspection."

On the drive back to Charleston, Carla was pleased at having accomplished this task. As an adult, she had learned to face an unpleasant reality rather than withdrawing into her inner world. For the first time in her life, she felt empowered. It was a good feeling.

Conditions did improve after the commander's visit. Shortly after Carla got back to the base, the major to whom she had originally complained abruptly disappeared from her assignment, without explanation. Base scuttlebutt said she'd been transferred, but those who knew for certain weren't saying. Carla, of course, had her own ideas and was more than pleased by the absence of the major.

The two male sergeants remained in the office, however, Carla no longer was harassed by them.

The end of Carla's enlisted time arrived, she had kept both promises. She completed basic training and she didn't fail. And, her clouded racist mentality went unchallenged.

Self-discipline and a taste of success lent courage to the deceptive belief that she was ready to reenter the civilian work force.

2

In Desperation

The old southern charm of Charleston, South Carolina, with its moss-draped oak trees and genteel antebellum homes captivated Carla's heart. Renting a room in Mary T's home, Carla decided to make Charleston her home.

Once again flung into the doorways of the market-place unprepared, battered about, and taking verbiage blows, Carla tried her hand at various jobs until she was awakened to the truth—her lack of qualifications. "Three years of military training is useless in the civilian market," she lamented.

"Carla, you're capable of doing better. God knows, your difficulty isn't from lack of trying, but from the lack of education. You must realize the importance of a good education," Mary T impressed upon her.

"All right, all right, I'll visit with the dean at the College of Charleston," she brazenly announced.

He reared back in his chair behind his desk and with a wide grin, he let her know, "Carla, your GED (general education) scores are too low for college work. You'll never make it. You have to complete a four-year formal high school first."

Impotently, Carla returned to her intellectual draught. Concluding a higher education was unreachable, she accepted a job operating a copying machine. Discouraged, she attempted to satisfy herself with the colorless world of disappointments. She had a nice gentleman friend, Matt, who was the special man in her life. For the two years she had known Matt, she felt comfortable with this nice looking, easy-going individual, he was fun to be with. She quietly assured herself all was well.

After a period of time, a new opportunity unexpectedly presented itself and Mary T brought it to Carla's attention. "The Catholic junior college is advertising that it's accepting several students in the Associates of Arts program. Carla, you really should consider it." A window was opened—not much, but enough.

"I would have to be boarding on insanity to even consider, or accept such a possibility of attending a Catholic school."

With Mary T's persistent persuasion, Carla relented and applied. She discovered the dean, Sister Mary Albert, was a kind and gentle person. A large, robust individual with rose-colored cheeks and penetrating brown eyes, she looked Carla in the eyes and in a no-nonsense tone, "Yes, your scores are very low for college work, but I'll give you the opportunity to try if you really want to." A back door opened, and Carla stepped inside. "Yes, I want to try," she was quick to respond. She had come to understand society's insistence of an education.

She was faced with finding the beginning of herself. Touched by the unseen inner force, she couldn't do otherwise. Circumventing the long-missing years without a good education to prepare her for college was a monumental challenge.

Sitting together, Mary T and Carla talked it out. "There must be a way to meet the challenge."

"We could try and find tutors to help," Mary T suggested.

"We can't afford that Mary T. I'll just have to teach myself what I missed during my younger years."

"Of course, you can do it. You can buy some used grade-school books from the neighborhood school," Mary T encouraged.

To this end, Carla moved in confidence to accomplish an arduous task. She incredibly delved into the child of her being, wandering in that inner world of safekeeping in order to study backward to go forward.

Upon entering the junior college she decided, "I won't look toward the end of the road, but I'll keep my eyes on each step as I take it. The key is to finish the work of each day. One day at a time, one semester at a time, I'll tend to my dream," was her motto. It worked.

Finishing a year at the junior college, Carla was accepted at the University of South Carolina in Columbia to earn a bachelor's degree in psychology. She would spend three summer sessions at the Citadel in Charleston.

With a steadfast purpose, and with Mary T's continual help, she attained the unreachable, a B.A. degree from the university. Finally, having bowed to society's demands, Carla felt well connected and home free. Vowing, "I'll never, ever, see the inside of a schoolroom again," she confidently sought employment.

Delighting in the sweetness of the seductive joy of trusting the system, Carla applied for and received a position in Charleston as a vocational youth counselor for the state of South Carolina. Filled with the joy of her good luck to have found the job of her choice, she passionately embraced the appearance of permanency.

The clouds of uncertainty soon materialized in the form of a rumor that the counselors were required to earn a master's degree. The state offered to sponsor a full year of study to reach that goal, but Carla was horrified. "Surely, this is the worst kind of nightmare. With my low S.A.T. scores and a poor background in math, it isn't within the realm of possibility," she protested, her face contorting with frustration. Mary T understood her young friend's predicament but could only offer a sorrowing expression.

The truth of the rumor was soon made clear when an area supervisor called her into a private office. Sitting on a chair just a few inches from the supervisor, Carla detected a firm resolve in the stern, clear-blue eyes confronting her. With no trace of the warm smile that had greeted her only moments before, the supervisor leaned toward her and said bluntly, "Carla, if you expect to stay in this field of work, you must get your master's."

Sinking back in the chair, highly irritated and believing she couldn't possibly stomach any more school, Carla retorted, "My grades aren't good enough. My educational background is poor. I'm not qualified to enter a graduate program. It can't be done."

Knowing Carla's educational background, the supervisor softly smiled and this time, in a gentle voice, she responded, "Ah, but you have always done such a good job of circumventing."

Horrified, Carla was quick to counter, "But I don't see any way out of this dilemma. How can I earn a master's degree in one year, a degree that usually requires two for those who are well qualified?"

"Just give it some consideration," insisted the supervisor. The supervisor was convinced there was yet an intellectual treasure buried in an unharvested mind. They parted and Carla was left with a horrendous, insurmountable task. She knew now that life's connections were made without permanent links.

"How can anyone ask this of me? Most people have bumps on the road of life. Me, I have mountains to climb. It just isn't fair."

Although Carla possessed an unsophisticated intelligence, she did have an uncanny way of accomplishing a task.

Silencing doubts, Carla lay awake at night worrying about the mandate. She convinced herself, "Sure, there must be a way to continue the intellectual progressive climb. There always is and don't I have to try something before I know if I'll fail or succeed? After all is said and done, isn't it the trying that's the real success?"

Thus stimulated, she pondered the essential necessity to find the path that would feed the unresolved insatiable craving for knowledge. Her supervisor had recognized this long before Carla had.

Instantly, Carla rose to a sitting position. She remembered hearing a co-worker discussing a graduate program at an all-black state college in Orangeburg, South Carolina, ". . . and with approval of the dean, the program can be done in one year." An idea began to form. "*Yesss*, perhaps there is a way of circumventing after all."

Carla had no hidden agenda. She wasn't out to change the structure of society; the selection of an all-black college was a purely selfish coincidence on her part. She believed the standards would be lower, the work doable.

Most of Carla's clients were blacks. She enjoyed working with minorities. She helped them to qualify for training and job placement. Remembering her own troubled past, she was better able to help them.

In Carla's white world, she labored under the misconception that all minorities really needed was training and encouragement. She overlooked the degradation that blacks suffered solely due to the color of their skin.

In truth, the work was more of an ego trip for her. She was constantly reinventing herself. The fact that they were black and she was white didn't play a major role in her scenario. Having never been held back because of the color of her skin, Carla didn't fully relate to the real problems that minorities were confronted with their entire lives. It didn't enter her racist mind that she was part of their problem.

The following morning from her office, Carla telephoned the dean, requested an application form, and casually mentioned she was Caucasian. He didn't seem to care.

Through the good will of the dean, another door was opened to her that if she chose, she could enter. It wouldn't be without a price but, for the moment at least, the cost was illusive. Her zeal for achievement pushed her ever more toward the outer world she had long retreated from.

Ah! Scarcely remembered was the "no-more-school" vow made only a year earlier. Carla hurried to greet Mary T with the good news. "I'm about to try the impossible. I'm about to try for a master's degree in one year? My parents will be so proud." Black was the least of her worries.

During this period, placid race relations dominated South Carolina's population of more than three million. Riots in Watts, Detroit and Newark were remote to this state, nestled in the deep south. ". . . The governor, all of us, had been very proud of the fact that we had no violence...."[1]

Located forty miles southeast of Columbia, the state capital, Orangeburg, with a population of 20,000, remained a bastion for

---

[1]Jack Bass and Jack Nelson, *The Orangeburg Massacre* (Macon GA: Mercer University Press, 1984) 33.

ultra-conservative whites. The city, however, was home to two black colleges, South Carolina State College and an adjacent private institution, Claflin College, with a combined enrollment of 2,400.

South Carolina State and Claflin college students had a history of standing up for civil justice and equality.

In 1956, a historically important black student movement began in Orangeburg on the campuses of South Carolina State and Claflin College. The movement that involved marching, boycotting, and demonstrations was significant because these well-organized activities preceded the better known Greensboro, North Carolina sit-ins of the 1960s by at least four years.[2]

In the early 1960s, the college students were active in the Orangeburg Freedom Movement, and by 1967-1968, the time was ripe for a new non-student activist group, Black Awareness, to form an alliance with the students. Unwittingly, Carla could not have chosen a more volatile hot spot for potential racial conflict than Orangeburg and South Carolina State College.

Within the week, Carla received the documents in the mail. She completed the application. It never for a moment crossed her egotistical, racist mind that she was about to tackle more than just a master's degree. Without the least thought of the possible consequences, Carla began a chain of events that would test her childish audacity for challenging authority—and her adult determination not to fail. Mount Everest rose before her.

It was a pleasant, cool, sunny morning at the end of May when Mary T and Carla parked close to the administration building. Carla's gait expressed the advantage she believed she had as she strode the short distance to the dean's office. It was two weeks before course registration. Walking up two short flights of steps, they opened a door with large letters: THE DEAN OF GRADUATE STUDIES OFFICE.

---

[2]Cecil J. Williams, *Freedom & Justice* (Macon GA: Mercer University Press, 1995) 97.

An attractive young black secretary greeted them. "Good morning, the dean is expecting you. Please, go right in."

As they entered, a tall, well-built, slightly bald black man, the dean, smiled broadly and courteously rose from his large polished wooden desk. Carla's attention was drawn to his large, dark eyes, boldly placed, and cheeks beginning to sag into jowls beneath circle-lined eyes. They revealed a kindness that she would come to appreciate. The mouth was strong and his expression was matter-of-fact. He welcomed Carla and Mary T and invited them to sit.

They each sat on one of the two large, overstuffed brown leather chairs in front of his desk and the dean sat on the front edge of his desk. In his right hand he held Carla's personnel folder. He glanced at the folder and with a twist of his wrist it moved to stir the air as he announced, "Your papers are all in order. However, I'm concerned about the burden of carrying an extra class load and the need to complete the degree in just one year." Carla was concerned about attaining a master's degree, *period*, so his warning was ignored.

Mary T discussed the concern they both had about the required statistics credit. "Carla, you can wait until your last semester to take statistics. You'll have had the necessary time to become adjusted to graduate work. We have an excellent professor who teaches statistics. You'll have no problem with it," he assured her in a convincing tone.

The dean made no allusions to her race. However, he offered her a private dorm room on campus for the summer. Carla quickly accepted.

As she left the office and briskly walked to the car, Carla noticed the meticulous planning of the gardens, the abundant greenery, and the tall, stately oak trees. Not at all what she had expected. It looked good enough to be a white school.

To keep her job, Carla gave little thought to the fact that she might be one white student among hundreds of blacks. The full impact of this decision wasn't yet registering. Being the only white graduate student on the campus meant being deeply immersed in "their" world, rather than dealing with them at arms' length while they were in "her world." Living in "their" dorm, eating in "their" cafeteria, attending "their" classes and otherwise interacting with black people in far more intimate way than she ever had before in her life hadn't penetrated Carla's tenacious mind.

The quiet, pleasant setting beckoned her. Carla's mind focused on attaining the degree. Exhilarated, her space here was taken for granted—on this campus, as the air she breathed.

Carla had little contact with blacks outside the work place. The chasm of separation yawned wide between them. And looking at the gardens, she didn't think about it. The pretentious calm in no way reflected the unrest displayed on campus a year earlier when students marched in front of the president's house, protesting faculty policy decisions.

Carla was utterly sure of only one thing—"I'll put every effort, mentally and physically, into it. I'll prove I can do it and the people who believe in me won't be let down." But what could she have comprehended? She had drawn incorrect conclusions from the phenomenal three-dimensional world she only had recently entered.

Her car packed, it was time to leave Charleston and Mary T. She would miss this trusting, caring friend. Then there was Matt, her gentleman friend. Their times together would be less frequent now. Carla hugged Mary T, and they said their goodbyes.

Pushing aside all doubts, Carla told herself that going seventy-five miles north wouldn't change anything.

Carla exited the interstate, drove a quarter mile, and made a left turn to the campus entrance. Grassy slopes holding large bold, white letters spelled "STATE COLLEGE" welcomed her. Immediately, Carla had a foreboding sense she was crossing an invisible line. Surprisingly, nothing seemed familiar in the place she'd visited only two weeks before.

Continuing her drive, Carla looked for markers to restore her sense of familiarity. Finally, she recognized the administration building. Then, on the right, the dorm in which she was to live—Annie Williams Woman's Dormitory, a recently completed structure that was shiny and inviting in its newness.

Parking in the lot directly across from it, Carla walked the short distance to its entrance and stepped inside. Walking halfway down a hall to the housemother's office, she was warmly greeted by an elderly face.

"It's strange to see a black housemother. It's different. It's something I'll get use to," she reassured herself.

The housemother instructed, "Please have a seat in the waiting room across the hall." Taking a few steps through an open arch, Carla stepped into a large, well-furnished room and sat.

Inside the room, several students conversations came to an immediate stop, as they became aware there was a stranger in their midst. Their conversations became less audible. Sitting on the edge of the seat and smiling nervously, the radical nature of her undertaking momentarily triggered an inner awaking. "I must be a surprise to them. It seems strange for my being here too. I hope I don't have to wait too long."

Fortunately, a call from the housemother interrupted her sudden insight. Relieved the spell was broken, Carla quickly answered the call. She was introduced to a young black woman who the housemother instructed to show Carla to her room.

Silently, they walked down a long hallway. Reaching Carla's room, her guide handed her the key and pointed to an exit at the end of the hallway.

"There's a parking lot at the side of the dorm. You can park and unpack your car easier from there." Having completed her task, the young woman appeared anxious to be on her way.

Watching her as she quietly retreated, Carla put the key into the lock and turned the doorknob. A pleasant room with a bathroom to her immediate right, two twin beds on the right wall, two single windows fronting the street joined the left wall, then a high dresser, and a long double desk.

She walked down to the end of the hall toward the exit door that the young woman had earlier pointed out. Opening a single door, she rejoiced, "Great, candy and soda machines. That's a familiar convenience." In front of her was a metal exit door with a crash-bar lock. Pushing her weight against it, she exited the building. Driving her car back to the side exit door, Carla proceeded to unpack.

Among the many boxes was a small reel-to-reel tape recorder. A friend had suggested that it might prove of value to keep a diary of her graduate school year. Agreeing, she thought a tape recorder would be the easiest method for posting events. Little did she know what a good and faithful friend she would have in the tape recorder.

With the car unpacked, Carla returned it to the parking lot. She retraced her steps back to the dorm and prepared for registration.

Now, with registration behind her, she was resting on a bed in a black student dormitory. She had made her initial entry into their world.

In an arrogant self-indulgence, Carla recorded how she really felt about blacks? "I know they're somehow not quite on par with other human beings, certainly not with whites—a part of society to be tolerated, but not wholly accepted. I'm here, after all, in desperation. Certainly, I never would've considered such a close association otherwise."

3

A Twisted, Warped Mind

Beads of moisture covered her forehead. She got up, crossed the room to the air-conditioning unit. It wasn't working. Her tired feet carried her to the dorm office and she reported the unit was out of order.

Within minutes after returning to her room there was tapping on the door. Opening it, there stood a middle-aged black man wearing blue overalls. "I come to check the air-conditioning unit." A polite man, but obviously surprised when he saw a white woman. Without another word spoken, he fixed the problem quickly, and was out of there within ten minutes.

Resting again on the bed, Carla thumbed through class cards, receipts and papers. Reaching for her meal ticket, her inert fingers allowed it to slip and fall between the bed and the side wall. The bed wouldn't budge, and she couldn't get her hand between the metal frame that was bolted to the side wall. Even with the mattress and box spring removed, she was unable to retrieve it. "Oh good Lord. Damn! What am I going to do now? I'll have to go back and admit to that black woman that I lost it the same day she gave it to me. Stupid! Stupid! The very thought of it is humiliating."

Wallowing in a vain disquietude, she was hungry, her throat raw. To placate the persistent hunger pangs, she decided to dine from the soda and candy machines that she earlier was so happy to see.

Her hunger momentarily satisfied, Carla showered and noticed her watch read 8:30 in the evening. Feeling drowsy and frustrated from a troublesome day of disappointments, she called it a night.

By 10:00 P.M., Carla hadn't closed her eyes. An accumulation of myths and false beliefs evoked hostile attacks. All kinds of horrible thoughts and pictures ran through her head and spilled onto her tongue. "That black repairman. He knows what room I'm in. What if he comes back? He probably had a key. He may even bring a few of his buddies. They were probably out there in the dark waiting." She was instinctively aware of the danger surrounding her presence. She considered running but knew they could easily catch her.

Having troubled and muddied thoughts that pervaded her mind, she fell into a bottomless pit of tormented darkness where vile fantasies produced forms born of the hatred of another race.

"I could be raped, beaten! I've heard about this kind of thing; they liked white women. At this very moment they must be whetting their lust and innate desire to have a white woman. Oh my God, my dear God. What am I going to do now?"

One hour later—an eternity. "They know where I am. They know I'm here alone." Demons felled her mind with memories imprinted coupled with the ignorance of time passing. She wanted to scream but believed, "No one would care. No one would help me. I'm all by myself here. The black women in the dorm won't help me. I've got to stay awake. That's what I must do. Mustn't fall asleep. I'll keep the light on. That may scare them away. Must stay awake. Must stay awake."

At 1:00 A.M. there were footsteps, noise and voices in the hallway. The footsteps faded, it grew quiet again. Carla didn't know which was more scary—the sounds or the quiet. Struggling with vile thoughts, not able to resist them, she produced fantasies of dark lustful carnal forms. She felt displaced and in the darkest corners of her soul. Intense fear pervaded her entire being. "Must not close my eyes. How will I ever get through this night? I'll get up and put cold water on my face. That should help me stay awake."

Another hour passed. Carla continued to talk to herself in a hushed whisper, "How will I ever get to my classes? I must get some sleep. But I dare not close my eyes." A vision of gang rape tormented her. "This is the time of morning they'll break in." She sat up on the bed in the corner, pulled her knees to her chest beneath her chin and wrapped her arms around her legs. This, she believed would prevent her from dosing off. With all zeal, she tended her desperate vigil.

She checked her watch. It was 3:30 A.M.—unrestrained, the fires of insanity intensified. With eyes heavy with sleep, she struggled not to close them. She was trembling and shuddering from the fear that burned into a mind held hostage. "How am I to protect myself? What am I to do?" She repeated over and over aloud.

In Carla's twisted, warped mind, an idea materialized. "I'll wrap my shoulder purse straps around the doorknob and push a chair under the doorknob with a stack of textbooks on it. This should work. If anyone tries to get in, I'll be able to hear them. Now maybe I can get some sleep."

But sleep wasn't on this night's agenda. At 6:00 A.M., still terrified senseless, she couldn't fall asleep despite her near total exhaustion and having barricaded the door to prevent the intruders from breaking in to rape and ravish her.

The first hint of daylight dispelled the night and the early sunrise lit the campus outside her windows, casting its light onto the street. However the light didn't penetrate into the dark corners of her mind, where the fiery shadows of would-be attackers resided. Carla realized she may as well get up and get ready for her early class.

She dragged herself up from the depth of hell where she had made her bed that night. With great labor she reentered the light of a new morning. Red-eyed, feeling totally miserable, her throat very sore, and wrestling with demons all night hadn't helped.

Nevertheless, Carla remained determined. She reasoned, "What a night! The longest night of my life. I must start the day anew—if only I can get my hands on a good hot cup of coffee. It is much too early for the dining hall, and I don't have a meal ticket. So, breakfast isn't possible. Coffee will have to do."

Dressing quickly, she hurried the three blocks from her dorm to the student center. The previous day's drizzle hadn't left any telltale signs. The grass was plush, walkways were dry and the roses sparkled from the morning dew. The student center was fronted with large glass windows and low steps extended its full width. A wide band of blue traced the top of the building's oblong front. Carla pressed her full weight and pushed hard on the unyielding glass door. "What's the problem?" She peered inside. The place was empty. Finally, she noticed a large sign hanging on the inside the glass door, OPEN AT 9:30 A.M. "Some beginning!" Feeling foolish, she looked around to see if anyone noticed what an idiot she was. Seeing no one, she quickly left.

Her first class was on the top floor of a three-story structure. As Carla approached, the building appeared to be suspended in midair. A large opened area was beneath its first story with a set of stairs at either end. The building was supported on each end by one-story buildings. Climbing the steps, Carla stepped onto a wide concrete landing that stretched to the assigned classroom.

Expecting a half-empty room, she walked through the doorway and stopped short. The classroom was full and class had already begun. Looking into a classroom full of black faces, all staring back at her, she tentatively walked in. With her heart pounding, the heat of her face blushed at being late. A professor asked,

"Which class are you looking for?"

"Practical Counseling,"

"Your class has been moved to another room," he curtly informed her. Thanking him, she quickly retreated.

A burning, raw throat, no sleep, and now she didn't even know where to go to attend her first class. She was going to be late for her first class. More frustration.

She noticed a well-dressed man who looked like a professor, walking the concrete landing. Carla approached and asked him if he knew where her class was moved. "I don't know, try the next building." Scrambling down two flights of stairs and into the adjoining building, then back up another flight of stairs, Carla found no classes in session at all. Down another flight of stairs and up some more. Still, no luck. Frantic, Carla was on the verge of missing her first class on her first day of school. If that weren't enough, her new shoes were rubbing a blister on her heel.

Completely helpless, lost and out of breath, she stood still. Another professor came along and asked, "Are you all right? May I be of some help?"

"My classroom has been changed and I don't know where to go." He smiled kindly and invited her into his office. Immediately, he picked up the phone and called the registrar. He let it ring a few times and then hung up.

"No answer, it's not open yet." With a grimace, Carla shifted her weight from the sore heel. He suggested, "Walk to the registrar's office and seek their help when they open." The problem was by that time, Carla would've missed her first class of the day. Thanking him for his time, she despondently left his office.

Returning to the now threatening stairs—the blood trickled, and Carla's heel stung sharply. Maintaining her composure, she refused to limp. Students were coming and going all around her.

Heading for the registrar's office, she crossed the square and came upon another large building. "Ah! I might as well give this one a try. I'm late anyway."

Pushing in the swinging door and walking down a wide hall, she passed music rooms with large square windows on either side of her. Students were well into their morning practice. From an open doorway, Carla saw a large classroom. She timidly walked to the door's edge and whispered to the nearest student, "What class is this?"

The male student looked up and whispered back, "Practical Counseling."

"This was it." Wearied and wounded, she entered. Through her tired haze, she saw a black professor standing behind a desk, speaking to the class. Before Carla could sit, the professor interrupted his talk, looked at her directly and said, "You must be Miss Mancari."

"Yes. I'm sorry for the interruption," she weakly muttered. She handed him her registration card and tumbled down in a front seat nearest the door. She felt safest near the open door.

Fifteen sets of eyes followed her. Not meeting their eyes in return, kept her from being overwhelmed. Tired, hungry and feeling displaced, Carla hardly heard or concentrated on what the professor was saying. All she could hear pounding at her inner ear was, "When, oh when, will it be over?"

"Be ready to start class first thing Friday morning," the professor concluded. Then looking directly at Carla, he added, "And please, all of you, be on time." She got the message. Then, "Class dismissed."

"Finally!" With a new found serge of energy, she quickly vacated her seat, and moved out of class without looking to her left or right.

With her first class behind her, a more serious problem was demanding her immediate attention. Carla's throat was intolerably painful. She walked a couple of blocks to a small structure that housed the infirmary. A brown face in a white nurse's uniform greeted her and upon hearing Carla's complaint ushered her into an examination room. Taking her temperature, she gave her a small envelope containing a half-dozen aspirins. Thanking her, Carla left with her wounded heel unattended. It was difficult enough to admit to one medical problem.

It was still too early for the much-wanted cup of coffee and an hour remained before her next class. She headed for the privacy and solitude that would only be found in her dorm room. Safely alone, she pulled off her shoe and slowly, and carefully rolled off the clinging bloody nylon that had rubbed the skin off her heel. Gingerly, she washed the blistered flesh and placed a dressing over it. As she propped the foot upon a pillow on the bed, she questioned which bothered her more, the pain, the hunger or the solitude.

She mumbled her disapproval of the annoying second day. "I may as well be in a foreign country—isolated, no one to talk with, not even a hello. Walking what seemed like miles this morning, lost at every turn, no coffee or food for two days. I'm shocked at the unfriendliness and the isolation, I miss seeing a white face." But it was time to put herself back together and get to her next class.

Arriving, she found the class also had been moved, this time to the auditorium in White Hall. She started to feel a little paranoid. "Are these changes somehow aimed at me, an attempt to test my endurance?" The logical part of her knew that notion was ridiculous, but the part of her that was beginning to be annoyed with the system wouldn't be silent.

"At least this time, I'm not going to be late," she consoled herself.

Painfully trudging across campus, Carla passed the side of a small grassy area and entered a path that curved. The distance was the equivalent of six city blocks, but seemed much longer. Finally, she arrived and smiled as she saw written in big letters on the building. WHITE HALL, "An ironic name for a building on this campus," she smirked.

Slowly she climbed the stairs. No speed was left in her. While she moved in slow motion, other students rushed past. Reaching the top step, Carla opened the door to the auditorium, entered and sat again nearest the door. Students began to file in past her. They left empty seats around her. Oh! How she wished she were home. The temptation was to get up and leave.

4

Humiliation

A tall, slender, well-dressed, good-looking professor pointed a brown finger across the classroom over the heads of the students. And warned, "A 'mino' is among us." The finger pointed in Carla's direction. Laughter filled the room.

"Mino" reverberated in Carla's head. The students understood the term and by implication, she realized it meant someone among them was different. The professor stated the obvious, a minority occupied a seat in his classroom. And that meant, of course, Carla was the "mino."

Owing to last night's hardship, Carla questioned why she was still here. Finding it wasn't a venture for the faint-hearted, a million questions gnawed within the crevices of her mind.

Faintly, over the laughter, the professor attempted to call the class to attention. A barrage of shrilled laughter sent a chill through the air that penetrated her questionable mood.

"Please be quiet and give me your attention," demanded the professor. "You're each here to become proficient in your field of endeavor. In my class, you're all abecedarians. To get that all-elusive 'A' requires a maximum relinquishment of your time and effort. And I expect it from each and every one of you."

"Wow! Abecedarians? What in the world were abecedarians?" Immediately, Carla nicknamed this instructor Professor Symbolic, since he spoke English very well and complex words were symbolic of him. Half jokingly, she made a note to herself to bring a dictionary to his class.

So began Carla's character naming of the professors. It wasn't out of a lack of respect, but rather a means of maintaining her emotional sanity. They were her private fantasy, her personal way of thinking about them, rather than modes of address. Carla used their proper names in classes, and never shared her personal nicknames for the faculty with her classmates. A sense of humor would be of the utmost importance if she were to survive at all.

"You have your reading assignment and the course outline. Be ready to start bright and early in the morning, and please be on time."

"Had my morning misfortune reached his ear? Not possible." In painful silence, she left the classroom. Carefully maneuvering the descending steps, she turned her glance toward the blue-banded building. "I want that cup of coffee now."

Six long blocks across campus to the snack bar in the student center separated her from the long-anticipated cup of coffee. Hurrying, her blistered heel reminded her just how long a walk it was.

Students milled about, walking to and from class, greeting each other. Exhibiting an assured sense of belonging, the other students seemed to feel quite at home.

No one passing Carla's way smiled, met her eyes or spoke to her. No one directly acknowledged her. They remained impervious to her existence. In every way, she was invisible, a non-entity. Several times during her walk to the snack bar, students approached her, walking three abreast. They walked purposely toward her while they pretended she wasn't there. They left no room for her to pass. She could either walk into them or be forced off the walkway onto the grass. Carla walked on the grass.

Her fellow students were blatantly telling her what they thought of her. She didn't belong here, nor was she wanted. Carla felt less than human. She unconsciously walked on the edge of the walkway, looked down at her feet, ready to stand aside to let others pass. Defeated and annoyed, she surmised, "Always walking on the grass. How many ways are there to humiliate me?"

Finally, climbing the low steps, she placed her weight on the wooden porch floor and pressed the door inward. Bordering on desperation, she entered the student center in hope of a hot cup of coffee.

Once inside, she paused a moment and looked around. She noticed the place was alive with activity. Four booths were filled with students engaging in animated conversation. Directly to her left was a long counter with a row of high stools. Refocusing on her intended purpose, she traveled the few steps and sat on one of the stools.

At first there were the now-familiar stares. Students at one table laughed and Carla assumed it was at her. Other than that, she was ignored. She felt terribly uncomfortable, still there was no way she was leaving without a cup of coffee.

Placing her attention directly ahead on the steel grill that leaned against the back wall, her eyes slowly moved until they found the coffee machine.

After an eternal twenty seconds, a young girl working behind the counter timidly walked over to where Carla sat.

"May I help you?" she shyly asked in a low voice, barely meeting Carla's eyes.

"Yes, please, a cup of coffee," Carla ordered in a soft but weary voice.

"To serve or to take with you?"

"To serve," she quietly requested.

"To take out?" The young girl repeated, believing that Carla had misunderstood her.

Not sure how to make herself any clearer, Carla tried another approach. "No. To drink here," Carla said emphatically, while touching the top of the counter.

The young girl quickly reached for a cup and saucer, walked to the coffee server, poured the coffee and returned. Her hands shook, and the hot black liquid spilled out of the cup and into the saucer. As she attempted to place the cup and saucer down before Carla, the cup did a momentary tap dance before it tumbled over onto the floor. With a clatter, the porcelain cup spread its parts over the floor. Everyone stared.

"I'm so sorry. I'll get you another cup."

As she attempted to set the second cup and saucer nervously before Carla, Carla realized, "So, we're both anxious."

The coffee's heat prevented her from drinking it fast. Taking several sips, Carla paid for the coffee and left behind the one thing she'd wanted most for the past two days. Once again she headed for the solace of her dorm room.

A short respite allowed Carla to regain her composure. The time had arrived for her to swallow her pride and hurry to the administration office to request a replacement for the lost meal ticket. It was a difficult task, but one she could no longer put off. The same individual who had issued the original meal ticket only two days earlier wasn't on duty. Thankful for small favors, Carla breathed a sigh of relief when her questionable story went unchallenged. She wasn't so sure she would've bought it herself.

Locating her third and last class of the day, the scene repeated itself. Although the room was soon crowded, she sat alone surrounded by empty seats. Carla noted, "Effectively, I'm not here. At the moment, I also wonder if I'm here. It's, alone again, alone again—I'm alone." Her heart was beating to an all-too-familiar tune. Surely, Carla and the other students were worlds apart.

The students were introduced to a medium large, somber-looking, elderly black professor. Like the other professors, he wore a suit, white shirt and tie. He took his place on a straight-back chair behind a small wooden desk at the front and center of the room. Because his somber expression never changed throughout the entire class period, she would nickname him Professor Serious.

"We'll work together whenever possible and learn together." He emphasized the "together," while he looked directly at Carla.

"How can I work together with people who won't even speak with me?" Carla questioned herself. Yet, immediately, she liked this man. He talked continuously for a full hour and, for this brief time, Carla stopped feeling sorry for herself. Forgotten was her physical discomfort and being alone. It was an interesting class and she was ready to learn.

Class ended. As hungry as Carla was, she still wasn't able to venture a visit to the campus cafeteria. She recorded, "Thinking I'm ready and actually doing the deed are two different things. My courage hasn't yet extended to deeds. I'm just not able to face eating alone and being ignored among a sea of black faces. I just had to settle once again for the gourmet offerings of the vending machines in my dorm."

After a tasty feast of peanut butter crackers and soda, Carla read her assignments for tomorrow. As she prepared for bed, the irrational terror of the prior night returned to claim her. It was much easier to be brave during the day, but as darkness cast its shadows, she was saturated with the fear of being attacked.

Tormented and anxious, she warned herself, "They're coming. They're going to attack. What am I going to do?" She set up her defense—the chair-under-the-doorknob, piled high with books, and purse straps wrapped around the doorknob. She decided, "This time I'm going to test it out." Placing a hand with fingers securely tightened around the doorknob, she braced herself for a difficult pull, and began to turn the knob. Z-o-o-p. To her horror, the chair moved quietly and easily, not a book fell.

Shocked! "Did this mean that I wasn't safe, after all, last night? I thought that I was protected. I give up. It's too much." She laughed aloud, "Dumb, dumb, dumb. Any other bright ideas? I'm a fool of my own making." Dismantling the doorknob contraption, she prepared for a good night's sleep.

The third day on campus was a repeat of the first and second. Subjected to a physical endurance test, she ate little and walked alone, mostly on the grass.

In self-pity, she surveyed her predicament and recorded, "Every part of me is hurting. The students are constantly testing me. A silent test, but a test just the same. I may as well be in a convent."

By lunch time, Carla's desire for hot food and coffee won out. "Lunch today would be the perfect time to brave a visit to the campus cafeteria." The cafeteria loomed before her with its wide sloping steps ascending to several entrances. In trepidation, she climbed the steps, approached an entrance, and entered a large dining room. A number of long tables with many chairs placed around each of them filled its space. Running the length of the left side of the room, the food was displayed in deep hot trays inserted into counter wells. The delicious tempting odor of long-awaited hot food enticed her to step forth and partake of the day's offering.

Obsessed with but one thought—hot food—Carla reached for a metal tray from a stack and picked up eating utensils. Entering the food line, for the moment, she was oblivious to her immediate surroundings. After having made several choices and filling a cup with piping-hot coffee, Carla turned toward a table where nine other students sat. They were laughing and having a good time. Captivated by the aroma rising from her tray, she walked to the table, said hello, and sat down with them.

No one said a word. First four, then three, finally the last two got up, their trays in hand, and moved to another table. They were telling her, "We don't want you on our campus. We aren't going to eat at the same table, talk to you or sit near you in the classroom. Nobody will."

Abandoned at a long, empty table in the cafeteria, Carla finally got the message. Dejected, she acknowledged, "Their actions are louder than words. They're declaring war and I'm the enemy. Now I know the many ways that I can be humiliated."

Crushed, her shoulders slouched, her arms went limp and her hands lay lifeless in her lap. Her heavy heart filled her gut. She observed, "I'm no longer hungry. It cuts to the core of my being. It hurts with every breath I take. The unbearable invisibility defeats me." Ego shattered, she left.

As she returned to the dorm, a misty liquid arose to flood her vision. Sobbing inwardly, Carla called it quits. She wanted out.Wearily, she packed books, clothes, and recorder into the car, and getting behind the wheel, she drove clandestinely off the campus. Like a prison escapee who may be stopped at any moment, she left her prison behind. "Now I know what that invisible line

was when I first drove through the entrance. 'Bars, black bars.' "
She tearfully informed herself.

Looking about, she noted, "I made it. I'm free. The ordeal is over. I'm in my predominantly white world." She rejoiced at the sight of white faces everywhere. She'd begun to think that there were no whites left in the world.

Thinking there was no time to lose, no one could convince her to return, she forcibly depressed the accelerator and took the quickest route. With a desperate need to know that the rest of her world was still intact, Carla hit the highway and sped home to Charleston.

5

A Gift

Hastily, Carla checked the rear-view mirror for cars. Nearly to Mary T's house, she reminded herself, "If they didn't want me on their campus, why would they follow me here?"

She pulled onto the unpaved strip, stirring the dust as she brought the car to a quick stop. Glancing toward the front door, Carla saw a stunned Mary T stood on the front stoop. The late afternoon sunshine highlighted her golden hair.

Carla greeted Mary T as if she hadn't seen her for years. A momentarily speechless Mary T finally broke the silence in disbelief. "What are you doing back so soon? What on earth is going on?"

With raw emotions laid bare, a reservoir of tears burst forth. As tears coursed down her cheeks, with quivering lips, and between sobs, Carla babbled incoherently. Mary T couldn't understand a word she was saying. However, the seriousness of the situation was obvious.

With great concern, she put her arm around Carla's shoulders to help steer her into the house. "Well, come in and we'll talk about it," Mary T said softly.

Entering the familiar surroundings restored Carla's sense of belonging. Even the pictures on the walls and large console television seemed like long-lost friends. It was so good to return to a known environment.

Mary T always listened. Carla was sure she wouldn't want her to remain in *that* environment. They passed through an opened archway that led them to a large dining and kitchen area. The round maple table with its four chairs were surrounded by large triple glass windows, allowing the natural light to fill the room. A picturesque view of the green grass and shrubs were easily seen. After Carla's few days of absence, everything seemed brighter, greener.

The kitchen with its almond-colored appliances was just a few feet away. Mary T moved toward the stove as she invited Carla, "Sit and rest a spell while I make dinner and a fresh pot of coffee. You'll like that, won't you?" Her soft tone soothed Carla's erratic breathing. The sobs came less often now.

Sitting at the dining table, Carla's muffled voice broke through the sobs. "Mary T, the students despise me and don't want me on their campus. The humiliations are insufferable."

"Carla, are you sure?" Mary T quietly inquired.

Of course, I sit alone in the classroom and in the cafeteria at a long, empty table. Students laugh and talk around me. And three students walk abreast defiantly toward me, forcing me to walk on the grass."

"Ah," mused Mary T.

"I'm *not* going back! I'm *not* going back. I am not changing my mind."

Gradually, after retelling her experiences in tears, consoling herself for over an hour, the sobbing quieted. Mary T simply listened. Carla's defenses were up, but she braced for whatever good sense Mary T could possibly make of it all. Instead, Mary T simply said, "Let's eat."

Finishing dinner, Carla cleared the table while Mary T made another pot of coffee. Mary T returned to take a seat across the table from Carla. Casting her eyes on the cup before her, for a long, silent moment, she fingered the cup and then looked up with eyes warm and intense.

"Carla," she began, "you've been through this before. Remember all the people who told you that you couldn't get through the university? But you did it, honey. You proved all of them wrong. That took you three whole years, but you did it. You can do this too. Why, you can do this standing on your head. Just take one semester at a time like you did before."

With the hot food and fresh coffee, Carla was content for the moment. She listened but said, "I don't believe it'll be quite that easy. It isn't the same. I can do the work. But it's the blackness. I never considered how 'all black' would be. It's horrible. Everywhere I go, everyone I talk to, nothing but black. I'm surrounded. I didn't realize how surrounded I'd feel. It's too tough. I'm alone. I'm unwelcome. I'm the minority. They don't want me on their campus in their world. And yes, it's their world. I'm invading their privacy."

Rising from the table, Mary T returned to refill their coffee cups. Taking her seat again, she cautioned, "Carla, stop feeling sorry for yourself. You're not the victim. Carla, you're walking in their shoes. You're experiencing what they experience every time they leave that campus. You're being touched by the heart and soul of another race. Consider yourself blessed. It's an experience you could get nowhere else."

"But I'm not looking for a blessing of any kind, particularly at South Carolina State." Mary T's unwavering demeanor reminded Carla she wasn't going to win this one. Exhausted, Carla had no fight left in her.

Talking late into the night, Mary T reminded her, "Carla, look how cooperative the dean is in allowing you to take the required courses in one year, to take statistics in the last semester so it'll be easier for you. He even arranged a private room in the dorm. You're so fortunate and you're not a quitter. Don't give up now."

Having pushed all of the right buttons, Mary T smiled as Carla vocalized her new-found determination.

"All right, all right, I'll go back. Oh, I'm only there to get a degree, not to make friends. They aren't going to force me to quit. No one can cause me to fail. These students aren't my life line. How then can they ever tug at it? They're not going to change my course. And, they will not change the color of my skin, mind or heart."

"That's my girl. It's late, time to get a little sleep. You must get up by 5:00 to drive back to school. You don't want to miss your first class."

Embraced by her own room and bed, her recent fears crumbled into a promised undisturbed sleep. It wouldn't be easy to rise in just a few hours, to leave the comforts of home and return to a room and bed she had so recently fled.

Glimpsing the well-manicured grounds at South Carolina State, Carla drove through the invisible line and headed back to class. As the bars silently clanged shut, she cautioned herself, "Once again I'm in isolation, solitary confinement. I have a choice. I can wallow in self-pity or get on with pursuing my degree."

During the next two weeks, Carla developed a routine: Attended every class, sat in the second seat of the second row, nearest the door. She wanted them to see that she wasn't afraid to sit among them. She sat in class in silence, aware that she was competing for human recognition.

Not ready to face a mass of rejection at mealtimes, she continued to avoid the cafeteria in favor of the vending machines. For someone to talk to, she turned to her tape recorder and expressed her feelings, her loneliness.

This routine allowed her to relax and to seep into the background. She began to survey the campus, well-kept with many of the buildings, including the U-shaped building in which two of her classes were held, were new. A library and a male dorm were under construction. Classroom floors were carpeted and the rooms well-lit.

The nights passed without incident, but from her deep-seeded fertile racist quagmire another vile demon was unleashed. During the early hours each Friday morning, Carla braced for a sinister walk to a nearby junior high school where her practical counseling class was held.

Walking the distance to the school took her through an isolated field past enormous shady moss-draped oak trees. The trees ran along the path for about fifty yards where a new men's dorm was under construction. The path then led to a fenced-in ball park. A gate was opened for students to enter.

Inventing attackers who hid within the fenced ballpark or behind one of the brooding trees, she placed one foot before the other, cautiously peering about her as she moved along.

As Carla crossed the field, one morning, a white construction worker was working on the new men's dorm. Delighted to see activity along the path and ecstatic to see a white face, Carla relaxed. White meant safe.

Greeting him with a friendly smile, she was hoping for a sign of pleasant recognition. What she saw was disgust covering his face, his eyes frozen in contempt. He brutally stared. If it were possible, she felt more unsafe. Not a word was spoken, but his defiant stare screamed, "Something should happen to you, bitch. You have no business here. You're worse than they are. Nigger lover! Nigger lover! Nigger lover!"

Carla retorted beneath her breath, "I can't offer any excuse for being here. The selfish reason is mine and mine alone. I won't apologize for stepping over the white line to get something I want more than his approval at the moment, nor will I allow myself to feel ashamed." She consoled herself, "Pity is the mother of self-destruction, as shame is the father of self-damnation. I'm not about to allow my soul or my mind to be born of either parent."

Meeting his disgusted gaze, she held her head high and turned her attention to the path before her. Eyes straight ahead, she walked with a determined step through the isolated field. Caught between black and white, the doors to both worlds closed against her. Pensively, she uttered, "Nothing would ever be the same again—nothing."

Arriving at the classroom, Carla took her usual seat as she awaited the instructor. Since her first class session, Carla liked this short, very dark-complexioned man with kinky, close-cropped hair sprinkled with generous amounts of white. He resembled an older version of Sammy Davis Jr. He wore glasses held by a wide, flat nose, and dressed immaculately. He, of course, would be called "Professor Sammy."

She noticed how dynamic, enthusiastic, and emotional Professor Sammy was about his lectures. He was in constant motion on his feet, as he waved his hands the entire class period.

"The black disadvantaged youth can't verbalize as can a white youth," he said, standing directly in front of Carla. He looked at her and spoke as if she were the only one in the room. "They don't know the words, Carla. They haven't had the opportunity to learn. You can't counsel them as you would one of your own."

The room was in complete silence. Feeling a blanket of stares, Carla sat still. She felt tested by him and the students. She was determined not to allow them to provoke a response. Not for a moment did she forget where she was. She resisted the childhood urge to spring to her feet and argue. She sat motionless. It was clear he didn't mean for her to respond, because Professor Sammy decided to teach Carla to understand the disadvantaged black youth. Carla decided, for the moment at least, that silence was golden. By the time the lecture ended, she felt like twenty-four carat gold.

Quickly, Carla was out of her seat and door, through the gate and across the dreaded field and on to the next class. Entering, she noticed a ring of emptiness around the second seat in the second row. They expected her to occupy it. Carla didn't disappoint them.

Professor Serious taught in his usual manner with no change of expression and no informal discussions. He was thorough and knew his subject matter well. The long, lonely hour passed. Next stop was Professor Symbolic's class.

After having been the butt of his pointed "mino" remark, Carla's first impression of Professor Symbolic was that he was out to get her. This morning he informed the students they would stand up and introduce themselves.

Swallowing hard upon hearing her name called, Carla yearned to flee, but stood instead. Wishing she was anywhere but here, she took control of her vocal cords to be sure there was no tension detected. "I'm Carla from Charleston, South Carolina. Employed by the Youth Opportunity Center in Charleston, graduated from the University of South Carolina and enrolled as a full-time graduate student here at State College." She didn't believe it was necessary to mention she was Caucasian. That spoke for itself. Now they all knew who she was, where she was from, and why she was here.

The introductions proved informative. Two of the students were also from Charleston. Carla was impressed with the attractive copper-complexioned young woman in her mid-twenties, Crystal, when she spoke of her educational goals with such conviction. The other Charlestonian, Norton, caused her to wench at this huge coal-black, barrel-chested man with a thick muscular fighter's neck who was in his thirties. Notable were his huge round face dominated by large, bulging, mesmerizing eyes and puffed cheeks. His appearance was frightening. Carla shuddered at the thought of meeting this man on a lonely street at night—or for that matter, meeting him alone anywhere, at anytime.

Like Carla, they were all graduate students. Most were teachers who taught during the fall and winter months. Carla noticed they seemed engaged in their class assignments and eagerly participated in class discussions. This was true in her other classes also. The level of their intelligence and their high motivation to learn was unexpected. They didn't seem to be any different from students she'd known at the University of South Carolina.

But she was also finding, to her surprise, the professors were more of a superior quality than she'd expected. They were knowledgeable in their subjects and presented themselves in a professional manner. It left Carla with food for thought. Of course, she hadn't, yet, made up her mind about Professor Symbolic.

After class was over Carla headed toward the cafeteria. Students continued testing her, walking three abreast and forcing her off the sidewalk and on to the grass. Ignoring the challenge, she smiled, and looked them straight in the eye as they forced her off the sidewalk. They laughed and smirked as they walked past. Carla convinced herself, "This is a beginning and I'm hanging on. Besides, I'm alone anyway, so what difference does it make if I'm on the sidewalk or on the grass?" Continuing her walk past the cafeteria, she glanced in its ominous direction. "I'm not yet ready to try it again. Soon, perhaps soon."

The end of another long, isolated school week arrived. Pleased that she had lasted two weeks, she felt there was a good chance she would finish the nine. To hang around for the weekends would be overkill. It was back to Charleston for a weekend of comfort, encouragement and, most of all, a predominantly white world.

Driving home, leisurely this time, her mind dissected the problem. The lack of trust was based on the color of skin. She didn't trust them because they were black, and they didn't trust her because she was white.

Surprisingly, she asked herself, "Why am I dwelling on this issue, the bars that separate us? Why do I care about these people? I'm in school to get a master's degree, that's all. I don't want anything else. But I do want my classmates to accept me. My outlook is changing. It is happening, and it's happening to me. And no retreat is possible."

Upon returning home for the weekend, Mary T listened and Carla assured her, "I'm doing much better. I'm handling my fears much better."

"I'm glad to hear you're learning to cope with the situation. You must learn patience, Carla. It'll take you a long way. Patience allows time to distinguish what we fear as it loosens its grip."

"Mary T, sometimes I think the barriers between the students and myself are impassable. There is so much disturbance within our beings."

"Disturbance is the undertow by which you may be pulled into the depth of your being for a greater understanding. It's the understanding that allows peace."

"Sure, but remember, it's the undertow that can also drown me."

"You've managed to swim through some pretty turbulent waters of life thus far, I think you can handle it."

Mary T laughed when she heard the nicknames Carla had chosen for the professors. "I'm sure they have a few choice names for you, too."

The sharing and laughter with Mary T was a calming influence. From here things didn't seem so bleak. Carla returned to start the third week of school.

It was very much like the first two. She walked, sat and studied alone in silence. She attempted to break through the barriers of resistance by looking directly into the other students eyes. She smiled and greeted them. She wasn't yet brave enough to tackle the cafeteria.

During the fourth week, the unexpected occurred. In Professor Symbolic's class, Carla took her usual seat and smiled at those around her.

"How are you coming with your outline?" asked a female student sitting directly across the aisle to Carla's right.

"Rough," Carla replied, feeling like a nun breaking a vow of silence. "How about you?"

Despondently, the chubby-cheeked young woman responded, "I just don't understand what he wants."

"I'm going to his office after class to look over some old outlines that he has on file. Want to come with me?" Carla smiled as she extended a warm invitation.

"Yes, wait for me after class."

Extending her hand out across the aisle, Carla introduced herself, "I'm Carla."

"Nice to meet you, Carla. I'm Wilma."

Professor Symbolic began his lecture, but Carla didn't hear a word he said. Her brain kept repeating, "Did I hear right? Did I hear right? Does she really want to walk over to his office with me? Certainly, I'll wait for her."

Class ended. Arms full of books, Wilma and Carla walked side-by-side down the hall to the stairs and out of the building to Professor Symbolic's office.

"I've always wanted to get an advanced education, but finances and the need to care for my three small children hadn't allowed it until now," Wilma shared with Carla.

"Just when I thought that my educational needs were behind me, I was informed I must have a master's degree to continue my work."

"It's society's needs that we're constantly being asked to meet. And as with any society, they're the needs continually change," lamented Wilma.

Passing a bed of roses, Carla was reminded how like a rose Wilma was. A rosebud of friendship that Carla hoped would grow into full bloom. She felt a sense of importance, a recognized individual, with Wilma at her side. Everyone who passed noticed them together. Carla wanted to shout, "See, I have a friend too. I belong!"

Climbing the few steps, they opened a door, and entered a small hall. A clerk directed them to the file with the research outlines. They made comments, notes, discussed the Professor's intent, and left the office.

Walking toward the women's dorms, Wilma informed Carla, "I'm staying in the older dorm across from yours." Knowing Wilma's quiz scores weren't the best, Carla seized an opportunity to help her with her academic difficulties and at the same time develop a budding friendship.

"Come to my dorm room later this afternoon and we'll study together for tomorrow's quiz."

"Thanks Carla, that'll be a big help. I'll be by around five."

Parting with a "see you later" and heading for their separate dorm buildings, Carla was in a state of euphoria. It seemed like such a small thing, and yet, it penetrated beneath her guarded heart to stir in her a peculiarly agreeable exhilaration. Her thoughts took flight, "Perhaps she'll even eat with me in the cafeteria."

With the summertime daylight brightening the room sufficiently, Carla carefully placed two chairs side-by-side in front of the double desk. Checking the materials, paper and pencils, all were ready for her first campus friend to arrive. As the room held an atmosphere of bubbling excitement, Carla could hardly wait for the appointed hour to welcome her new friend.

5:30 P.M. Wilma hadn't yet arrived.

5:55 P.M. Still no Wilma. Carla convinced herself, "She's coming. Just going to be late, that's all."

6:10 P.M. Carla worried, "Did something happen to her?"

6:30 P.M. Carla continued to wait.

7:00 P.M. And wait.

8:00 P.M. Dusk arrived, but not Wilma.

9:00 P.M. Sitting alone as darkness filled the room, Carla's expectations were just as bleak.

Feeling let down, she didn't understand and wondered, why, why did she care so much? Why did it hurt so much? Quietly, she recorded in the darkness,

> A moment of kindness is a gift that remains with the receiver and the giver, all the days of their lives creating a rippling affect that touched the lives of others. The power to penetrate minds of steel and hearts of stone breaking through years of resistance, kindness was all invasive. Kindness begins without an end. It's the most powerful tool man has in the universe. Its effectiveness so underrated, its use so sadly neglected.
>
> Wilma had for a moment at least crossed the bridge of human kindness. Our souls touched for one brief moment. When this happens, the Christian ideal of the brotherhood of man in the sight of God is realized."

Today, Wilma gave Carla just such a gift. And it would remain with her all the days of her life. She reached out to the light switch and, by herself, studied for the next day's quiz.

6

Breakthrough

The morning light brought into full view last night's disappointment. The undisturbed chairs remained side-by-side. Like salt being rubbed into exposed wounds, the raw memory cut deeply into a heart wounded many times in the past four weeks. For a moment, Carla deliberately closed her eyes in the hope the entire scene hadn't existed. But it had and she had to rise, dress and prepare for the morning classes—the first of which Wilma would also be present.

Wilma avoided Carla's inquiring glance. Wilma didn't speak to her. Her melancholy told Carla that she felt badly about having stood her up.

"Didn't we tell you to stay away from her?" They were talking about Carla. Wilma was rebuked by her closest friends for consorting with the "mino." She had betrayed "her own kind." Carla understood. It was difficult, if not impossible, to buck peer pressure.

Carla's heart bled. Beaten, like a washed-out rag, isolation closed in on her. Her fellow students were taking their collective rage at the entire white race out against her. Mary T's words echoed, "You're walking in their shoes."

"Well, they're tight, and they hurt."

Sufficiently humbled by the past week's events, a full sit-down hot dinner and coffee called Carla to the dining hall. The machine snacking left her hungry for a good hot meal. Would she do it?

Carla made her way to the stack of bright metal trays and placed one on the supporting rails. She set utensils wrapped in a white paper napkin on it and pushed the tray down the line. Quickly, she selected the food and a hot cup of coffee. Scurrying to a long empty table, she carefully removed a chair from the table's edge and sat down. Feeling well tucked in, she placed the napkin on her lap and with eyes cast down, she attempted the task of getting the food from the tray into her mouth. Fork-to-food-to-mouth. Coffee cup-to-mouth-back-to-saucer. Fork-to-food-to-mouth. Coffee cup-to-mouth-back-to saucer. An ordinary, matter-of-fact routine event required a major, deliberate and controlled effort. She experienced every bite, every movement in a dreamlike state. When would she wake up from this strange and perplexing dream?

After a few bites, Carla raised her eyes, glanced a little beyond the table, and cautiously, she peered about. Two tables away, four students were eating and exchanging friendly conversation. To her left, a table away, sat several other students engaged in laughter. They continued their activities as if she didn't exist.

Instantly, she returned her eyes and attention to the food before her. Finishing the meal, Carla rose from the chair, picked up the empty tray and carried it to the cleaning station. She was careful to perform each movement as though she was comfortable with the isolated, rejected, surrounding atmosphere. All the time her insides were screaming, "Get the hell out of here before you do something stupid, like drop the tray or trip over your own feet."

Carla quickly retraced her steps through the dining hall doors to the pathway that took her the two blocks back to the dorm and the welcome seclusion of her room.

She kicked off her shoes and dropped her guard. With a deep sigh, she collapsed upon the bed, realizing the monumental task she had just put herself through. Although Carla was feeling a bit pleased with herself for having seen it through to the bitter end, she realized for the first time what blacks experienced in a hostile white world. She shuttered at the very idea. She was aware just how drained she felt. It was a different way to go through life.

Grimacing, Carla speculated, "One year is hard enough, but a lifetime? One year for me, but the years go on and on when you're black. They need to be very strong—strong where it counts, within the fiber of their being, their very souls. How else can they take daily abuse and rejection? I can't pretend to be that strong.

With the passing days, Carla was haunted by another problem. Professor Symbolic and Professor Serious, she believed, were prejudiced against her because of her race. She believed that they didn't want equality for minorities, but rather they sought to overcome and rule over the white race. It was time for a visit to the dean's office. Perhaps he would help her to sort this out.

This was the first visit to the dean's office prior to registration. The dean smiled easily and spoke in a soft, jovial voice. It helped put Carla at ease.

Carla stammered, "I want to discuss ah-m my classes," his brown skin dislocated her thought processes.

"Carla, I'm pleased with your progress but you may be trying to do too much, too fast."

"Dean, really, I can handle the class work. I want to tough it out."

"Okay, Carla. Remember, it's all right if you decide to drop a course."

In the quiet of his office, his easy manner tempted Carla to discuss her dissatisfaction with Professor Symbolic and Professor Serious. But the necessary courage didn't rise to the occasion and she left the dean's office, putting it off for another day.

Returning to her dorm, she reasoned, perhaps she wasn't yet ready to discuss the racial issue with the dean. Since the Wilma incident, there was no question, she found she was sorting out her own racial feelings and how they were being affected. She had found, to her surprise, she actually empathized with Wilma. Carla saw herself in Wilma, which shocked her. Wilma shared the experience of wanting to belong. What else did she share? Could it be that they had the same feelings, wants, and desires? Blacks were just as human? "No!" It hurt her brain to even think about it.

Reluctantly, she recorded, "It couldn't be the same for them—no, it just couldn't be. Good God, my academic work needs concentration. Changing the social order, something I don't fully understand, shouldn't clutter my mind. Understand? I really don't understand them; we don't understand each other."

Carla wasn't ready to accept the equality of blacks. To do so was to deny the deepest and most fundamental definitions of the world and her place in it. To accept them as equals meant to express active concern for their well-being. It meant association with them off campus as well as at school. It meant bucking her own long-held beliefs, as well as rejecting the culture that she lived in. She wasn't ready to assimilate the realizations that poured forth from her heart. She wasn't ready for a transformation of herself and how she related to their world—a segregated world. It sounded super-colossal. It was too much.

She side-stepped the issue neatly by assuring herself it wasn't advisable to entertain such repugnant ideas. It was all she could do to keep up with her class assignments. Her studies actually took a great deal of her time and emotional energy.

Professor Sammy required taped counseling interviews, research papers, a good deal of outside reading and panel discussions. Professor Symbolic had her going in circles, spending days and many evenings in the library. He kept her in cold fear of not being able to please him. And that was only two out of five classes she was attending. So much for the class work being easier than the University of South Carolina—the idea was not proving true.

She managed to stay on track with her studies while at the same time getting used to the cold stares. A few of the students became a little less hostile. Some students acknowledged her with a few words of recognition. It wasn't much, but it allowed Carla to believe in time they would come to accept her on their campus.

Carla started eating dinner regularly in the cafeteria. It was less crowded during the dinner time. She still couldn't brave going there at lunchtime. No one sat or talked with her. On the occasions when there were no empty tables, she took a seat with other students. The ice was cracking. The students no longer left the table. It was an improvement. Still, she guarded against high expectations.

The two professors continued to trouble her. Carla felt discriminated against because she was white. Their anti-white comments increased. Unabated, the professors' lectures were about how bad whites were making it for the black race.

Carla was the center of class attention when the subject was discussed. The students turned in her direction to catch her reaction. She didn't react. It was odd for Carla to sit there and listen in full control of her youthful urge to challenge the speaker. Perhaps that was her secret, she wasn't there to challenge but just holding on.

At the end of the fifth week, Carla decided another visit to the dean's office was necessary. She believed she had the courage now to discuss her racial concerns. As she entered the dean's office, he rose from behind his desk and greeted her with a smiling glad-to-see you expression.

"Carla. Come in and sit a spell."

"Thanks for seeing me," she said, a little down-hearted.

Carla sat in one of the familiar overstuffed chairs directly in front of his desk.

"How are you doing, Carla? Are you having any problems?" the dean questioned, as he sat to her left in the other chair along side of her. His demeanor was relaxing, but she had the distinct feeling he understood exactly why she was here.

Carla took a deep breath and cautiously began,"Professor Serious has me worried some. I don't think he likes me. I never know where I stand."

Turning his body toward her, his right elbow rested on the chair's well-padded arm. His bold dark eyes met hers, and he spoke in a low, calm voice.

"Professor Serious has been around a long time. He's a distant and removed man. Even I can't get close to him. I'll admit he has some old-fashioned ideas about what education should be. But he is excellent in his field. Really excellent."

Not knowing quite how to respond, but not ready to confront the dean with the racial issue, Carla decided to take an indirect approach.

"I'm having trouble with my research outline."

Instantly rising from his chair, the dean walked with energetic steps to the shelves of books that lined the right side of his office wall. Quickly he found the one he was looking for. Removing it, he returned, sat down and handed it to her.

"Take this and read it and then go to see Professor Serious and discuss your difficulties. I'm sure he'll help." As the dean was about to rise from his chair, Carla's courage rose.

"There's something else." She said, a quiver in her voice. "Yes?" He sat back down and looked at her with those kind, expressive eyes.

"It isn't just Professor Serious. Anti-white remarks are being made in the classroom by a couple of the professors. I'm very uncomfortable about it."

Taking a deep breath and letting it out in a long sigh, he said, "Carla, you have to understand. These classrooms are some of the few safe places blacks can speak out about these issues. To speak of them in the outside world is to be perceived as being hostile. It allows the issue to be honestly addressed and it permits the students to let off some steam. Cooling off here may keep them from boiling over out there. Can you understand that?"

"Yes. I think so."

"And please consider this. Perhaps you're being oversensitive. Perhaps the remarks aren't directed toward you at all. Perhaps they're merely statements of truth as the professors perceive truth. Perhaps you're the one who is overreacting to ideas you aren't used to hearing and a point of view you aren't comfortable having expressed."

That hit home with her and she nodded her head. "I'll give it some thought, and I'll try to work with Professor Serious, rather than being at odds with him," she quietly affirmed.

Her worries about Professor Symbolic hadn't abated, but she hadn't wanted to appear weak, so she got up from the chair, book in hand, and thanked the dean.

It was late in the day when she left the dean's office. She felt somewhat better. The dean wasn't one to use many words, but he was always quick to reply, always to the point. She liked him; she had from the first time they met. She never thought of him as a black person, but just another person—one who seemed interested in her as a professional. Carla hadn't wanted to beat a path to the dean's door. She wanted to make it on her own.

With the dean's words resonating, she walked to Professor Serious's office in a corner of the gym. The door was part-way open. Looking up from his papers, Professor Serious stood, offered her a chair at the side of his desk. She accepted, and timidly began to discuss her research outline problem. Taking time to explain and clarify what it was that she was doing wrong, she found that he was surprisingly pleasant and courteous—even friendly.

She was put at ease and after discussing the academic questions, the conversation drifted to general issues. Unexpectedly, he began to talk about himself.

"I own land in another state. I have a dream to someday build apartments on it for blacks. Orangeburg doesn't have nice apartments for blacks."

Hearing a hurt tone in his voice, she pondered, how could one so accomplished and respectable as Professor Serious have difficulty finding quality housing?

Her facial expression betrayed her.

"That surprises you?"

"It does."

"Where are you from, Carla?" She wanted to say from another planet. That's exactly how she felt.

"Charleston."

He smiled, "I go there often. A lovely city."

Not prepared to cope with the unexpected conversation, Carla thanked him for his time and left the gym for her dorm.

As Carla entered the dorm, she did a double-take when she caught sight of her friend Marti's white face, light blue eyes and blond hair. Her appearance reminded Carla that there really were no bars blocking the entrance. It was a public institution.

Marti was a young co-worker from her job as a youth counselor in Charleston, one who was forever having romantic problems. Carla was always the good listener, friend and confidant.

"Marti!" she joyfully exclaimed. "What are you doing here?"

"Carla, I've been waiting for you. I need to talk."

Walking the hallway to Carla's room, Marti was quiet. Behind closed doors, Marti hissed, "Carla, you in a nigger dorm? I can't believe it." The word bounced about the room and pierced the walls.

Although troubled by her friend's language, Carla's only response was, "It's hard to believe it myself." Haunted by the recent conversation with Professor Serious, Carla sucked in her breath to cover her remorse, Marti sat on the center of one of the single beds, she folded her hands in her lap, tears coursing freely down her pale cheeks. Carla sat on the other bed directly across from her.

"Steve has left me," she moaned. "His mother, she treats him like a baby. She won't let go."

"Have you talked about it with him?" Carla gently asked.

"Yes. He said that if he makes her angry, she'll take away his car."

She was crying so hard Carla wondered whether she could see her through the flood of tears. Carla's insides retched. Her problem couldn't compete with what was going on in Carla's own world.

"Does he want to try and make a go of it with you on his own?"

"Oh, Carla!" she wailed. "I love him so! I don't want to live without him!" Tears continued to flow freely, and a heart was breaking before Carla's eyes.

Marti and Steve had been in a torrid love affair for the last six months. Until Carla left for Orangeburg she had lived the ups and downs with Marti and knew every little detail of their rocky romance.

"What do you want, Marti?"

"I need to move near him. But, I don't have enough money." Carla nodded.

"How much do you need?"

Writing a check, Carla reminded her friend that going away was all right, but running away wasn't the answer.

"Take care of yourself. No matter where or how far you go, the problem may not go away."

Marti dried her eyes with a handkerchief retrieved from the pocket of her petite pink cotton dress. With the sobs coming less often now, she took the check. They talked for about an hour, about Marti and Steve and also about the office, but Marti didn't ask about Carla's life at South Carolina State.

Promising to repay the loan as soon as possible, Marti walked toward the door, opened it, and suddenly she whirled around and said, "Carla, I can't believe that you're actually here. I would never do this for anything in the world."

With a forced smile, all Carla could say was, "Goodbye, Marti."

What Marti didn't realize in the past five weeks, Carla had said the exact same thing to herself. Carla, I can't believe that you're actually here!

Lying awake in the darkness of her room, Carla was reminded there were black and white people in this world. When she was here, she forgot there was an "out there." How about the students? How did they feel when they left the campus? They seemed happy here, free to express themselves. Carla was experiencing two different worlds, black and white, for the first time in her life, Marti's tears became hers and she wept. Carla felt so insignificant between the turmoil of human emotions, and so very worn by the demands for her attention.

After a fretful night's sleep, she prepared for the dreaded walk to Professor Sammy's class. Attending his class wasn't only a learning experience, it was entertainment and also very valuable. Professor Sammy usually had a lot to say. He was her favorite professor.

This morning he was in top form. He entered the classroom and immediately had the entire class enthralled in an emotionally charged lecture.

"You have to listen with more than your ears," he said, "more than your five senses. You have to listen with your entire existence. You have to be here."

His energy level rising, his passion for his subject grew as he paced the front of the classroom, speaking at the top of his voice while pounding at the center of his chest.

"There's more to being alive than just breathing and sitting in a chair for your clients. Much more." Now he was pounding the podium for emphasis.

"Realize that what people carry inside of them, they may not always be able to communicate in words. The spoken word isn't the entire thought. You must be aware of every movement, every expression, the body, everything." His words were rapidly pouring forth. "You must be ready to accept, understand, become the other self whenever necessary! You're only a counselor, not a god. You can neither perform miracles nor can you judge. But at least you can understand."

He made so much sense. Forgotten for the moment was his color. Carla saw a teacher whom she respected and admired. Suddenly, she remembered "the issue" and she was amazed. "How can anyone so black make such good sense?" she marveled.

"Do you understand?" he asked. "You must feel it, not just talk it or listen to it. Feel it. Rapport is a feeling, not a definition. You must make them want to come to you.

"I have a brother," he said, more calmly, "who once said that teaching is like singing. If you're going to move them at all, you must make them feel as though they could get up and come to you. Counseling is similar. It won't be what you say, but how the client feels what you say that will make the difference. Anyone can sit and listen to another, but you must communicate by also hearing what is not said."

Carla was impressed. He was so dynamic, so knowledgeable about his field. He gave her an entirely different view of the counselor's involvement. She always enjoyed the process of counseling. Now she wanted to really understand, the total comprehension that can only take place in the human heart. She was eager to return to counseling and to put into practice the lessons that Professor Sammy was teaching.

As the exciting hour ended, a female student from behind her leaned forward, smiled and asked, "Where are you staying?"

"In the Annie Williams dorm," Carla replied. The student smiled, and moved on. The end of the fifth week of school left Carla with the belief that there was the beginning of a breakthrough, a fine crack in the wall of Jericho. She also felt a sadness when she learned Wilma had dropped out of school.

In the beginning of the sixth week, there were also encouraging signs of change. Professor Serious spoke less and less about the "poor Negro." He was even at times apologetic for some of the things he said about whites. The visit to his office proved helpful.

While visiting with Mary T, Carla said, "The dean was right about him. He is good in his subject matter: I'm learning a good bit from him and I'm glad that I took the dean's advice.

"On the other hand, Professor Symbolic's class presentation assignment has me in mortal dread. I don't look forward to standing before an entire class of black students. I feel as if I having to ask for their approval. In my wildest dreams, I never envisioned that it would ever come to this."

"You've worked hard on your assignment. Preparation is more than half the battle. You'll get through it," Mary T assured her.

The big day had arrived and Carla climbed the two flights of stairs leading to the class.

She took her usual seat. Professor Symbolic was doing his usual number, prancing around and reviewing the morning's schedule. He informed the class two students would be giving class presentations, Jordan and Carla. He called on Jordan to begin his presentation.

Carla could hardly concentrate on Jordan's presentation. Butterflies were rattling her inner cage as she struggled to simulate an outward calm.

"Miss Mancari, you're next." The order catapulted attention to the work that she had to perform.

Slowly rising from her seat, she walked to the front of the room, turned and faced the students, petrified. Hoping they weren't aware of just how frightened she was, she swallowed hard.

The first few seconds were the most difficult. Once she rediscovered her voice, she proceeded to deliver her well-prepared presentation. With new-found energy, her voice became strong and clear. She was able to connect with her audience as individuals—not with just an appearance. It was a new and exhilarating experience for her.

Concluding her presentation, Carla thanked the professor and the students for their attention. She moved quickly back to her seat, took a couple of deep breaths to restore her composure and thanked God it was over. Then the question rose from within. Did she really care what they thought? The obvious answer followed. Yes, she did care. She really did care. Professor Symbolic thanked both students for their presentations and dismissed the class.

Nervously gathering her books and papers, Carla stood on shaky legs and removed herself quickly from the classroom. Firmly grasping the rail for support, she descended the two flights of stairs to the street level. It was a hot summer day. She couldn't be sure if the beads of sweat rolling down her forehead came from the day's heat or from what she had just been put through in the classroom. No matter, she needed the consoling space of her dorm room.

As she turned and took a few steps toward her dorm, a commanding male voice called, "Carla! Carla!"

She hesitated for a moment to assure herself that her frozen brain wasn't playing tricks on her. Again, she heard, "Carla." Baffled by the unexpected sound of her name, she turned around and saw Norton hurrying to catch up with her.

He was so large, so ferocious-looking, and so black. Holding her breath, she expected the worst. "Lord," she muttered, "what could I have done to offend him?"

"Carla, I just want to tell you how good I thought your presentation was."

She managed a pitiful, "Thank you," and in a grateful confusion turned again toward the dorm.

"Carla, would you like to join Crystal and me for lunch at the cafeteria?"

With her arms full of books, she attempted a full turnabout. She hadn't noticed Crystal standing beside him. Had the sun gotten to her? Were her ears and eyes malfunctioning? Was she suspended in midair, and had she died and gone to heaven? It seemed to take an eternity before she got her lips to sputter, "Y-ye-yes. Sure."

Norton's large puffed cheeks spread wide, his thick lips parted as he grinned with delight. As they walked the few blocks to the cafeteria, he told her of his and Crystal's weekly commute from Charleston to attend class. His voice was deep with warm intonations. His large bulging eyes softened, as he told her about his lovely wife and their new baby boy, their first.

They ascended the steps to the cafeteria together. Carla's delirious state of mind caused her not to be fully conscious of anything or anyone but the two individuals on either side of her. They entered the cafeteria, moved to the food line and made their selections.

Norton led the way to a long, empty table. Within minutes, other students joined them. Everyone wanted to say something to her. Friendly laughter filled the cafeteria space. She felt strange, yet comfortable. She ate the best meal she had in more than five weeks.

After lunch, Crystal and Carla walked in the direction of the women's dorms. Crystal asked, "Which dorm are you in?"

"The Annie Williams."

"Hey, that's my dorm too. What's your room number? I've some materials that may help you with your next assignment. I'll bring them to you later this evening, if you would like?"

"Yes," this time Carla's "yes" was jet propelled, no hesitation! They entered the dorm and each parted for their perspective rooms.

Later that evening, she skipped dinner to be sure not to miss Crystal's arrival. Carla didn't want to do anything that would cause her to miss her first student visitor to her room.

Four hours passed. Carla reminded herself, "I've done this before." Then convincingly she stated, "She'll come by."

A knock on the door.

"Come on in." Carla said casually as she could.

"I hope I'm not disturbing you."

"No. Not at all. Please, come in."

Handing Carla the promised papers, Crystal said, "I can't stay, I have to go, but I'll see you tomorrow in class."

Eagerly, Carla reached out and accepted the papers extended from Crystal's brown hand. Carla thanked her and watched as she exited from the open door.

The white of her teeth sparkled and her copper skin was as smooth and shiny as tinted glass. Her name fit her well, and this hand of friendship would not be withdrawn.

Carla's Christian consciousness was disturbed. The pieces of her beliefs no longer fit perfectly. There were ragged edges she had not yet recognized. Edges that tend to force a tear, a tear that could unravel the best of plans.

7

Hope and Friends

"If Norton says, 'She's okay, she's okay.'"

With the veil of suspicion lifted, the entire environment at South Carolina State College was pleasantly different from the previous six weeks. Weeks of rejection and isolation came tumbling down as expressions softened, lips parted in smiles, and students gleefully chatted with Carla. She was eating with her fellow students, joining in their conversations, and walking on the sidewalk. Norton and Crystal waited for her to eat at the cafeteria with them and other students always joined them.

Tacitly, Carla had learned a valuable lesson—don't judge by appearances. The very person who she would be in fear of meeting alone at night had taken her under his protective wing and showed everyone she was all right. As it turned out, Norton was popular, very well liked, and the top man on campus.

And, thanks to Crystal, Carla was accepted in the dorm. Finally, she was getting to know the women students in her dorm. Her neighbors, young undergraduates who planned to become teachers, were a delight to be around.

Upstairs, Thelma and Marie, close friends since their early childhood years, shared a room. Not only were they supportive of each other, but they invited Carla to eat dinner in the cafeteria. In their forties, substantial and dark-complexioned, both women had children and taught during the regular school year. Carla saw Thelma as the serious one, who wore round, clear plastic-framed eyeglasses. Marie had quick laughter and wit.

They had both sacrificed to receive their higher education. Thelma said, "I spent the first half of my life raising my children. I plan to spend the second half raising myself. My husband laughs at that but he supports my aspirations." Carla liked that.

Marie teased Thelma, "You have it a lot easier, you have only two children. I have four."

"Four? It's more like five. Your husband is the biggest baby you have," Thelma corrected her friend.

"You've got that right," laughed Marie.

Envying their closeness, it reminded her how distant she was from her own white world of close friends. Carla identified with their struggles for a higher education. Enjoying their friendship, Carla knew change was happening.

However, some things never seemed to change. Professor Symbolic continued to take potshots and digs at the white race whenever the opportunity presented itself. One morning he was discussing human relations and the difficulties of communicating. "If whitey can't communicate among his own kind then how can you ever expect him to communicate with the black race?" Carla felt the comment was directed at her.

As he continued to prance about with his well-chosen diatribes, Carla unconsciously cast her eyes toward her lap and, turning her hands from palm to back several times, checked to see if they were still white. This seemed to be happening more often lately. Immersed in their blackness, she was losing her sense of whiteness. It was as though she had to reassure herself that her color wasn't changing, black didn't rub off. Discovering she was still white, she was glad. Class was dismissed.

As Carla studied during the evening hours in the dorm, she heard the students' conversations. She realized they too had hopes and dreams. Hearing them talking among themselves in the hall and in the rooms, she was aware they weren't just another color, but they were living in another world.

She talked with her mechanical friend, "They have hopes as I have, but in their thinking and planning, they separate themselves from my world as if they know, even if it wasn't by choice, it's going to work out that way."

Their hopes are restricted, not by their talent and ability, but by their skin color. Hope! It is a potent life energy, ingrained in the human condition. If thwarted, it becomes a relentless destructive force."

At times, their speech was fast. When they were excited, she didn't understand what they were saying. Her inability to pick up on their pattern of speech held her interest.

The eighth week of school brought an unexpected closeness with the students. Her dorm room was a meeting place for group discussions concerning class assignments—and for socializing. The students seemed to enjoy being with Carla. In their conversations, they were more open and sharing.

Leaving the dorm for the early-morning class, Carla took in the exhilarating cool air of the middle of August. The grass was still green and the oak trees cast giant shadows. The campus was quiet, undisturbed by the many students who would soon be gracing its walks.

Abruptly, her thoughts were interrupted by the hum of a car motor. Turning, her eyes rested upon a smiling Crystal.

"Hi, Carla. Want a ride to class?"

"Sure, thanks." It was always a relief not to walk by the dreaded field.

"Nice car. It looks new," Carla casually remarked.

"It is new. My mother just bought it and would you believe, I get to drive it for a whole week."

"Great! You'll be able to get off campus a while."

"Yeah, I want to go to town and do some shopping. I have to get the car back to Charleston this weekend."

Surrounded by the smell of the car's newness, they chatted as Crystal drove. Arriving a little early, Crystal parked under one of the large oak trees fronting the classroom. Switching off the engine, she turned toward Carla and looked directly into her eyes. There was a painful despair in her dark eyes. "Can we talk?" Crystal asked.

"Yes, of course."

"Carla, why is the black race being refused the same privileges and opportunities you have? Why do white people think they are better than black people?"

Carla resisted the temptation to clasp at her heart as it skipped a beat. A solemn mask covered Crystal's usual smiling face. The anguish in her voice told Carla these questions came from a deep and profusely bleeding wound.

There had been a time when Carla believed she knew the answers to these questions. She had entered State College believing in her race's superiority. With the summer session almost behind her, she was beginning to realize she knew none of the answers. However, she did know if she were black she too would ask the same questions, with all of the hurt and pain she was witnessing.

In the past couple of weeks, Carla had engaged in a close friendly conversation with her fellow students. She thought she had managed successfully to avoid this kind of conversation. But here it was, and Carla struggled to respond as honestly as possible without hurting Crystal.

"Crystal, I couldn't honestly at this time answer your questions. But why do you think it's this way?"

Crystal looked away for a brief moment and then turned again toward Carla. With the soft, gentle voice that Carla was accustomed to, she spoke barely above a whisper. "It's fear of the white child mixing eventually with the black child. It's a fear that if a white and black child grows up together, they may learn to love, and yes, even to marry each other."

Knowing in the deepest part of her being that this may very well be the concern of Carla's race, she asked, "Is that what the future generations of your race actually want?"

Crystal wasn't angry. She answered honestly.

"Yes, Carla. Not only what future generations want, it's what we want now. We're good enough, why should we be totally rejected? Why should a black mother think, 'My son isn't good enough for a white girl?' Why, Carla? Why?"

Silence was Carla's only answer. Crystal's eyes were moist. It was painful for her to reveal what was in her heart. She continued, "I'm not saying it's going to happen that way. But what I *am* saying is why should it be prevented by law or prejudice. Yes, we want total commitment that we'll be totally accepted—and not just in schools, but on the job, in restaurants, in public facilities of every kind. We expect to be accepted as human beings, not someone who you turn your eyes away from or someone you have to work next to because that is the law. Yes, we want it all."

"Carla, do you realize that we can't use the local bowling alley in Orangeburg, and that to this day there are separate waiting rooms at the doctors' offices and at the hospital?"

That was news to Carla, but then she never had given it any thought. She never had any need to. Crystal wasn't quite finished. She meant for Carla to fess up to her demons.

"How do you feel about it, Carla?"

The question was straight-forward. Carla gave the only truthful answer she had at that moment in her life.

"Crystal, I have mixed feelings. My own beliefs have been challenged the past few weeks." Indeed, in the furnace of trials, Carla's beliefs were daily being mortified.

The gravity of the situation was profound. These two individuals, one black, one white, were walking on heaven's edge and dared to peep in. For a moment, Carla lowered her eyes, raised them and wearily added, "I do believe things will change. I do think race relations will improve some. They have to. However, I don't believe the totality of racial prejudice will be erased in my generation, I'm afraid—perhaps in the next, but not in my time. All we can do is work toward a better world."

Crystal turned away from her. She stared off into space over the steering wheel through the shiny windshield, a soft moan escaping her lips.

Now that the subject has surfaced, Carla risked a question of her own. "Crystal, will you answer a question I've had on my mind for a while?"

Returning her glance toward Carla, she softly smiled and said, "Sure. What is it?"

"I've been noticing the different shades of blacks' coloring. You mostly congregate together according to your shades. The darker with the darker and lighter blacks with the lighter ones. Is this also a carry-over—friends you mix with, ones you have in your homes away from the campus?"

Crystal reflected for a moment before answering. "You know, you're right! I've never thought about it, but we do tend to select the lighter shades if we are lighter ourselves. It's strange. The very thing that we're complaining about the white people doing to us, we're doing to each other." Her mood lightened. "Well, we surely are learning from each other, aren't we?"

Smiling, Carla agreed, "Yes, we certainly are."

They headed off to class together with a friendship cemented in honesty.

Later, the morning's conversation with Crystal replayed in Carla's mind late into the night. Crystal's questions continued to taunt her. They gave birth to new questions, causing Carla to wonder aloud, "What am I afraid of if I'm so superior? How could blacks threaten me? What made a person or a race 'superior?' Could it really be the color of skin, the texture of hair, the size of nose or lips? Is appearance really that important? Is it the determining factor of my humanity?"

Suddenly, feeling small and ashamed, Carla realized she hadn't the power to make such judgments. Carla couldn't sleep. Her very existence was challenged and her beliefs were crumbling before her eyes. Picking up the pieces and putting Carla back together again might not be easy. It might take a very long time.

Early in the morning, a soft knock on Carla's dormitory door pulled her away from the soul-searching. Thelma's usual pleasant and cheerful face was unexpectedly somber, a match for Carla's somber mood.

"Hi, Thelma."

"Are you going to breakfast?" she asked.

"No, I've an early class and plan to pick up a cup of coffee to go at the student center."

Entering the room, Thelma squinted and raised a hand in good gesture as she put on her best street-talk accent. "Girl, you should eat more. You so skinny your bones rattle a tune."

She was right. Eating, after all, hadn't been one of Carla's favorite pastimes for most of her weeks on campus. Laughing, Carla enjoyed the black idiom.

"Where's Marie?" Carla asked. It's unusual to see one without the other and Carla was curious why they weren't together. Thelma's face dropped even further.

"She had to drive home yesterday. Robert requested her presence." Her tone was both bitter and concerned.

Carla hadn't known the two for more than a few weeks, but when Thelma called Marie's husband by his formal name of "Robert" instead of Bob, something was definitely not to her liking.

"I hope it's nothing serious," Carla anxiously stated.

"Serious? I'll tell you what's serious. Bein' married to that man—now that's serious. Child, that worries me."

Thelma grew pensive. The street talk disappeared in a wink of an eye. "Robert likes his liquor hard and, when he has too much, he's abusive. Marie insists that it doesn't happen often. But I know better."

"I'll tell you what let's do." Carla comforted her. "If she doesn't return to school by late afternoon, we'll call her together, all right?"

"Okay," a somewhat relieved Thelma agreed. "Wait while I run upstairs to get my books so we can walk to class together."

A few weeks earlier, the students had distrusted and disliked Carla, but with this spontaneous invitation she sighed. She was part of the student body, a friend. A moment of warm pleasure washed over her.

Marie was fine. Early in the day walking the campus, arm-in-arm together, Marie and Thelma grinned and waved as Carla hurried to the library.

The ninth and final week of Carla's attendance at South Carolina State summer session found her without enough hours in the day. Spending most of her time preparing for final exams and completing research papers, she skipped dinners to keep up. Much of her time was spent in the school library.

It was late one evening when she left the library that Norton came running toward her. He was all smiles as he yelled, "Carla, wait up. I've something to show you."

"Hey Norton!" Carla called out. "What's up? Did you finally get that elusive 'A'?"

"No, nothing like that," he laughed. "I have some pictures of my baby to show you."

Sitting together on the library steps, Carla unloaded her books and joyously reached for the pictures. Together they flipped through about thirty pictures. The pictures showed a three month old with long legs, thick arms and, beautiful dark eyes.

"That's my wife Lori holding him."

"He's adorable, Norton. You must be enjoying him very much." Norton's large white teeth sparkled as he proudly said, "He's our first, so you know we have to spoil him." They both agreed and laughed aloud.

"What are you doing on campus so late in the day?" Carla asked.

"Finishing touches on a term paper, needed library time."

"I know what you mean. Just spent three hours in there—a research paper for Professor Serious. Hope he likes it."

"Carla, I had him last summer. He looks and sounds more threatening than he is."

"That's good to hear."

Norton hesitated. His large thick lips momentarily tightly pressed, fingering the baby pictures within his huge black hands, he looked up, and his piercing dark eyes captured Carla's.

"Carla," he tenderly asked, "are you returning for the fall semester?"

They had never discussed her traumatic first six weeks of the term. But now, sitting here on the library steps next to him, she saw that Norton understood the pain and anguish she suffered through. Inquisitively, he looked at her.

"Yes, I plan to finish the entire school year."

Their eyes met. With barely parted lips, her smile joined his. She could almost hear his warm heart say, "I'm glad," and her grateful heart responded, "Me too."

Without a further word between them, they parted, waving goodbye as if they were the oldest and most intimate of friends. Carla felt a twinge in her heart as she watched this huge muscular black man climb the steps of the library. She thought, what a lesson dear, sweet Norton continued to teach her—one of the most important lessons of her life. His gentleness, buried beneath his bulk, covered a tender, sweet soul. And, she had wrongly judged him by the color of his skin.

Carla had time for one last visit with the dean before the end of summer session. As she sat in the reception room waiting to see him, she reflected on how much had changed since the first time she entered this office. And, she wondered, if she had changed so much in nine weeks, what would the twelve full months bring?

The secretary signaled for her to go in. With his usual warm smile, the dean rose from behind his large well-polished mahogany desk. "Good to see you, Carla. Please, have a seat." Carla sat on one of the chairs directly across from his vision. The dean sat back down behind his desk in a tall back dark leather chair that swivelled back and forth. He leaned back and said, "Carla, you'll need to find housing for yourself for the fall and spring semesters." Carla was aware there was no space for graduate students in the dorms during the fall and spring semesters.

"That shouldn't be a problem." She reassured him.

He leaned forward, hands clasped on the desk top, and warned her, "Don't be so sure. If the local people know you're attending *this* school, you will not find a place to rent in Orangeburg."

Making light of the moment, Carla joked, "I'll wager you a dime I won't have any trouble finding a place to rent."

"All right. I'll take that bet. This is one bet I hope to lose," he confessed with a broad smile.

Then the dean became much more serious than Carla had seen him before. He stiffened in his chair, his brown fingers momentarily traced the front edge of his shiny wood desk. With a steady gaze he began, "Carla, do you realize that you'll be a marked woman for the rest of your life—a black mark? Your attendance here will be part of your record and your life, no matter where you go. There are those who will hold it against you."

With all that had transpired recently in Carla's life, she certainly hadn't considered that aspect of her experience here. It caught her by surprise. She had no ready response. Nodding, she rose from the comfort of the well-stuffed chair, she extended her hand and accepted his firm handshake. His voice less foreboding, he smiled slightly and said, "See you in a couple of weeks." Thanking him for his time and assistance, Carla left.

As Carla walked toward the library, for some last-minute studying, her head swam. The dean's mind-provoking pronouncement and the seriousness in which he said it clogged her ears tossing her into an unexpected tizzy. Her mind struggled to put it in some proper perspective. The ramifications were clear. We're accountable for every action taken, whether we're fully aware of it or not. Carla wasn't prepared to deal with the possible implications of the dean's statement. For the moment, at least, she must calm her frenzied nerves and focus her full attention on the finals.

On a bright cloudless morning, Carla left the dorm to attend the last class of the session. As she scanned the campus, she was proud of herself. She hadn't quit. An upbeat feeling enveloped the entire campus. Carla joined the black masses, one with them at last.

The day was filled with goodbyes. Once seen as a turbulent threat, the "sea of black" waters were calm.

"Well, girl," Thelma in her usual cheerful street slang, "you get some home cooking in you, you hear?"

"Thelma thinks everyone is too skinny." Marie chuckled.

"Okay, Thelma, y'all take care of each other."

After hugging and saying goodbye, Carla watched them walk away. What nice people they really were.

Sharing a warm farewell with Norton and Crystal, Norton reminded her, "We won't be back for the fall semester but we're looking forward to seeing you again for the spring semester."

"I'll miss you both next semester," Carla assured them. Deep in her gut, Carla wanted to return, to interact with her friends.

Taking a leisurely drive to Charleston, scenes from the summer days at South Carolina State flashed before Carla's eyes: the loneliness of meals from snack machines, walking on the grass, and that god-awful first night.

Puffed up with her own sense of accomplishment, she was pleased that she did well in all of her classes. She glossed over her new-found friendships. The students shared their lives with her and accepted her. A little uneasiness still quelled in her heart. The passing thoughts stirred. Was she the conqueror or the conquered? Where do blacks belong in our society, separate or as equals? She would be back in the fall. Carla's education was just beginning.

8

Empathy

"No niggers live here, you can be sure of that," the skinny, short, balding apartment manager bragged. Carla was faced with a little man who was dressed in a tieless white shirt and navy blue pants held by a well-worn black leather belt. He appeared to be in his late fifties. Squinting bespectacled eyes, pressed lips and a pencil-thin mustache foreshadowed a repugnant attitude.

The refreshing month of September 1967, had arrived, and with it the fall semester. As he waved his hands, he repeated, "There will never be a need to worry about niggers in this apartment building."

The stench of racial hatred filtered throughout the lobby of the four-story apartment building, only a few blocks from South Carolina State College.

Carla's urge to puke was successfully repressed, as her silence approved his bigot opinions. Although ripped with guilt, she wanted the apartment more than a confrontation about race relations.

"Who do you work for?" he inquired.

A red flag instantly went up. She vividly recalled the dean's words. "If the local people know you attend South Carolina State, they will not rent to you."

"I work for the South Carolina State Employment Office."

All she had to do was not volunteer additional information and, of course, hope that he didn't ask for any. That wasn't dishonest, was it? Cringing inwardly, she played mental tricks with her integrity to right a blatant wrong.

"Ah, sure I know where the state employment office is downtown. Would you like to see the apartment?" He extended his hand to a key hanging from a hook just inside his office.

"Yes, I would, please." Holding her breath, she hoped the inquisition was over and, please God, no more "nigger talk."

The little man blew his nose into a large white handkerchief and, as he pushed the elevator button, he continued with his "hate-niggers" discourse.

"No ma'am, no niggers to bother you." Involuntarily, she shivered. "I'm particular about who I rent to. All nice white folk here." Without skipping a beat he added, "For how long will you need the apartment?"

"About nine months."

"That's fine." He continued to impress her. "I know you'll like this place. It's quiet, good-sized efficiency and reasonable rent."

Stepping out of the elevator on the second floor, they entered a narrow hall. Walking a few feet, they stopped before a gray wooden apartment door. Inserting a key into a round, bulb-like brassy doorknob, he opened the door.

They entered a large room with a galley kitchen to the left. To the right, a round, wooden kitchen table with four wooden chairs. Directly ahead was a large picture window. In the expansive view of the parking lot, Carla could see her car.

To the right of the window, a studio couch that would serve as the bed, with a small wooden table at one end graced with a brass-based lamp. Across the room, an overstuffed chair faced the studio couch.

To the left of the window was the entrance to the bathroom, followed by a clothes closet. Shiny, black and white-speckled linoleum covered the floor and the entire apartment had been newly painted in white, creating an atmosphere of lambency.

He was right, Carla liked it. It suited her needs perfectly. He grinned. Another white for his whites-only apartment house.

Returning to his office, Carla filled out the necessary forms and paid the first month's rent and security deposit. She willingly betrayed her black friends for the need of an apartment. Given the opportunity to rise above her own shallowness, she complied with small minds, ignoring her conscience. In this duplicity, she was the loser.

Three months earlier, had this little wretched man bragged to her about excluding blacks, she wouldn't have thought a thing about it. Deeply disturbed, her experiences at the college had affected her off-campus life. Carla didn't know if that was good or bad. She did know that her insides were left with a distasteful, sinking feeling.

Professor Serious's remarks during her visit last session went off in her head as a three-alarm fire bell would.

"In Orangeburg, there are no nice apartment houses for blacks." Now, she understood why. With a reckless disregard, she pushed past that and reminded herself the apartment was perfect and in an excellent location. What she wanted was paramount to his culturally inflicted pain.

Leaving the lobby a traitor, she pushed the heavy glass entrance door open, and gratefully breathed in the fresh air. A few feet away from the entrance was her overly crammed car. She proceeded to relieve it of its extra weight and settled in her new home.

Feeling smug about how everything had fallen into place, Carla drove the few blocks to the campus for registration. This time, the large, bold letters on either side of her car, "STATE COLLEGE" read like a great big "HELLO, welcome back Carla, glad you're here."

Conscious of crossing the invisible line, she drove through. She entered a different world. This time, she was happy to be back. She had looked forward to seeing her friends.

Driving to the now-familiar gym for registration, a lighthearted Carla stepped out from the car onto the paved walk leading to the rear entrance. The beautiful clear, cool morning gave no hint of what awaited her behind that large wooden door.

She was sure registration wouldn't take too long. Smiling, she entered the gym. This time, the sight of all black faces didn't upset her in the least. Completely enmeshed in an intoxicated stupor of overconfidence, Carla moved forward.

Her mood was suddenly transformed into an instant downer. No one responded to a smile, nod, eye contact, or the return of a "hello." In a cold panic, she searched for a familiar face. None was found. Quickly, she moved to cover the distance between the entrance door and the long lines of angry faces.

Flustered and confused, Carla mustered what little courage she had left, steadied her feet, and entered a long line. Raw imaginings slowly rose to the surface of her memory as she slipped into a protective hypnotic state.

In spite of the hostile glares, Carla managed to register and, as she swiftly attempted to retrace her steps to exit, she heard several defiant comments.

"What's that white bitch doin' here?"

"She must be lost, man."

"She better get her white ass out of here."

Once outside, Carla hurried to her car, leaned against it and took several deep breaths. This one act of emotional and physical immensity had completely obliterated her egotistical complacency. Looking around, she was aware that the students on the campus were all new to her. There were many more students than during the summer session. She didn't recognize any of them.

Multiple questions filled her fever-pitched brain. She feebly muttered, "Am I back in hostile territory? Is this possible? Is everything I've been through and have accomplished during the summer session down the drain? Am I to repeat the isolated, depressive, deathly afraid and unbearable experiences all over again? It's inconceivable! Please God, no!"

She held fast to her slipping mind. Still, there was the bookstore to be visited. Entering the administration building, and descending the narrow stairs to the bookstore, she braved another long student line. Carla said a silent prayer that it would be different. Looking about, she knew that it wasn't. The anger, suspicious looks, distrusting expressions were all for her benefit.

She wanted to shout, "Hey! It's okay! It's me! I was here last summer. I made friends. I'm okay, really I am." But the cold stares and sullen looks prevented so much as a whimper from escaping her lips.

Finally, the clerk contemptuously asked, "You want something?"

Timidly, Carla handed her a book list. For an instant the clerk glared at the list then back at Carla with the expression of disbelief that these could possibly be for Carla. She thumbed through the list, reluctantly removed the books from the well-stocked shelves, and handed them to her. Carla handed the clerk the money. Not a word passed between them. She had done this before.

Reeling with despair, Carla sought the refuge of her car. Trembling as she inserted the key into the door lock, she opened the door, and hit the seat hard. With incredulous disbelief, she immediately locked the door and in agony said, "What's happening to me?" Then, to reassure her sanity, "This is only a temporary setback. Tomorrow, classes will begin. I'll be again with my old friends in the graduate classes and listening to familiar professors. Yes, tomorrow has to be a better day. It has to be." Starting the car, she scurried off campus, repeating to her numbed senses, "Sure, it has to be."

A week later, Carla was back in the grips of reality. She had five classes. The only professor from the summer session was Professor Symbolic. So, of course, she bitterly recorded her reaction on her tape machine. "If for any reason the students wanted to get at me, they couldn't have chosen a better weapon than Professor Symbolic. All new students, all new black faces and all new names. All their respect has to be earned again. Again, I must prove my human worth.

"I hadn't the slightest idea that I would have to go through it all again." Struggling to restore her thoughts, it boggled her mind. How naively foolish she felt, having believed that all the battles could've been won in just a few weeks. "I'm still a slow learner."

The graduate classes were held in the evenings, with the exception of one on Saturdays. The student body now was quite different then it had been in the summer session. Most were undergraduates, young, vibrant black men and women. Some of the graduate students were also younger than those in her summer session. Again, she was an outcast. She didn't belong in their world.

Recognizing that she had lost the ground she had gained last summer, she was also faced with a greater battle. Flipping on the recorder, she said, "This new emotion I'm experiencing is stronger and more piercing than the rejection I suffered during the summer session. That's strange, since I'm living in a white area off campus. This loneliness cuts deeper. It goes far inside of me to a place that can't be reached or touched. My heart breaks so from it that I'm sure if it wasn't for my soul, my mind would surely flee.

"I believe this will be one of the most valuable experiences. Certainly no one, not even my Creator, would ask this of me without good reason. Yes, I feel sure I will re-win the same old battles that were won during the summer session. But I'm not so sure with this new one. For it is a part of my existence, my essence. To paraphrase an old Chinese proverb: From victory little is learned, but from defeat much is learned. Defeat is fast becoming my middle name."

As Carla struggled to understand what was happening to her, an abiding, persistent feeling within her wanted to reach out to touch another, but her reach was too short. "Perhaps," she recorded, "one day, another would come along, stand before me with just such a loneliness, feeling that no one could possibly care or could understand. Then my reach will lengthen and I will touch another human being. Can I ask for more? I think not."

As the first week of the fall semester ended, Carla called on the dean. At least the attractive young secretary recognized Carla. It was a good reality check. She motioned for her to go right in.

The dean stood to greet her from behind his large wooden desk. "Hi, Carla! Good to see you back. So, tell me, did you find an apartment off campus that you like?"

"Yes, I did, and you owe me a dime," she replied smiling.

The dean laughed, reached into his pocket, brought forth a palm full of coins. He fingered through the coins for a dime and handed it to her.

"This is one bet I'm more than glad to lose," he said, as he took his seat behind the desk. Then the dean cautioned, "Carla, you have a heavy class load along with your part-time employment. You may be trying to do too much, too soon."

"It's all right, dean, I believe I can handle it."

"Okay, but if you have any problems, please let me know. I'm sure we can work it out together."

"Sure, thank you."

Carla shared with the dean the location and the niceness of the apartment, but not the circumstances under which she rented it. Her silence while the apartment manager bragged about his contempt for blacks was the heaviest load she had to carry this semester. She thanked the dean for his time and left his office.

Expecting the instructors to be weak and the standards lower than at the University of South Carolina, the quality of education at South Carolina State continued to astonish Carla. The professors were well-educated and top notch in their fields. Just one more myth exploded in her face. Conditioned racist attitudes died slowly.

One evening course had a most gentle professor. A serene calm presence exuded from him, causing him to be nicknamed Professor Good. Tall, with a large build, he was quite well-spoken and an excellent teacher.

Professor Good was absolutely wonderful! He was the kind of man one felt terrific just being around; goodness overflowed. He patiently explained everything thoroughly. Carla felt free to ask questions. He seemed to enjoy answering them.

Another evening-class instructor she called Professor Sorry. He was always saying how sorry he was for the "poor Negro." Tall, broad-shouldered, and had a thin-line black mustache, he too was an excellent teacher. Unlike Professor Good, Professor Sorry was obsessed with the disadvantages minorities faced.

The third and fourth professors were pretty much average-looking. They made incidental racial remarks once in a while.

And, of course, her fifth professor was Professor Symbolic. He continued to be a conceited ass. He was more wound up this semester than he had been during the summer. Fired-up about black issues, he spent much of the class time discussing them.

It was during the second week that Carla came to understand what it was that was causing the great abyss of loneliness that she felt. It wasn't hers; it was theirs.

She wished that she had adequate words to describe it. It was so within her that she couldn't yet fully express it. Mary T had described it best when she warned, "Carla, you're being touched by the heart and soul of another race. Consider yourself blessed." Mary T, so wise, so intuitive.

"This, of course," she recorded, "was why I could never win this battle. It's not my fight, but theirs. It's their great loneliness that I feel. Theirs, perhaps, in trying to reach me or reach the white race. I'm but a symbol of it on the school campus.

"The cold stares, the drawing-near, then pulling back, all along they were trying desperately to say something. Understanding now, I feel much better. It's as though a great weight has been lifted from my heart, which once again belongs to me."

The students' stares began to soften as they started to accept Carla on their campus. Their trust was slowly being earned and Carla gradually felt comfortable in relationships with them.

She shared with her mechanical friend, "I feel such a great empathy for my classmates. I want so much for them to know that I understand, especially now that I too have felt it. I'm sure that the one thing, we all want is to be loved as human beings, to be loved and accepted as human beings—then all else would follow."

9

An Act of Kindness

September had brought the beginning of shorter days and longer evenings. Its pleasant breeze smelt of bubbling, erupting emotions, as the humidity dropped and lent rise to a higher level of energy among the students.

The small groups milling around seemed strange, out of place. Many were men that Carla didn't recognize as part of the student body. Subtle and now not so subtle changes were taking place on campus. Preoccupied, she shrugged off the strange scene. The hours of studying and reading ahead of her flickered across her mind as she approached the library.

Gradually, as the semester progressed, Carla inched into the good graces of her fellow students. Perhaps the change taking place within her was a silent communicator. They began to work well together in the classroom, and three of them formed a study group with her.

James wore his hair in an afro; his medium height, slender build with fine features made him look more like an undergraduate. A mouth covered with a boyish grin tended to give him a mischievous appearance. As the class comedian, the appearance read him well. If anyone looked sad in class, he would send a written smiling-face message. James never had to sign it; everyone knew who it was from. He made them laugh. Another member, Arnie, was tall, dark, lean. He had the look of a lawyer with his metal-rimmed glasses and his close-clipped hair. He always had to have the last word and was very popular with the girls. Lil had fine etched, features. Petite and light-skinned, she was very pleasant, even-tempered, and took her studies seriously. All three were in their twenties.

They met in the conversational area of the library. A couch, several large wooden chairs with thick cushions and a long low wooden table, used to support their books and papers, accommodated their needs.

James often complained about his father. "Dad thinks college should be all work and no play, and I believe it should be mostly play and a little work." James lived what he preached.

"What college did your father attend?" Carla asked.

"What college? He has five years of school, total. The rest of his life has been all hard work. He's so proud that I'm working on my graduate degree. I can't disappoint him." James really wanted to do well and make his father proud.

As the four of them studied that first afternoon, Clayton, another classmate, spotted them and came over and joined the group. Tall and muscular, Clayton was a soft-spoken, well-mannered young man who always addressed Carla as "ma'am," making her feel a hundred years old. She liked Clayton and she was glad he joined them. James' friend Smitty dropped by and chatted with James briefly about a meeting they were to attend later in the day. Smitty was a sophomore, tall, lanky, with a well-defined mouth. His hair was thick but well-shaped, and his large dark hooded eyes had a dreamer's look. He was a handsome, articulate young man who was very involved in the civil rights of the students. Carla admired his energetic commitment to his fellow students.

Smitty's short visit reminded Carla of the conversation she had with Crystal during the summer session. "Carla, do you realize we can't use the bowling alley?" It had been news to Carla and it had contributed to a sleepless night.

After Smitty left, the group returned to its free and open discussion of their class assignment. No barriers or walls were felt. Carla noticed how much they were like the white students from her undergraduate days. Their color really hadn't made them different in the content of their thinking and actions. Two hours passed quickly. A lot was accomplished and they agreed to meet weekly.

In a taut class atmosphere the following evening, Professor Good informed the students, "A new organization, 'Black Awareness Coordinating Committee,' is organizing on campus. A black man named Cleveland Sellers, not a student but from a small town twenty miles from here, is heading the group.

"In loud, demanding voices, some of the younger students insist 'the brothers and sisters' join their militant ranks and fight for 'the cause.'"

With a troubled frown, he continued, "Despite the fact that they haven't yet engaged in any overt activities that could be considered unlawful or violent, I'm quite disturbed about what's happening on the campus.

"The group is writing objectives. They meet every Monday evening and have a guest speaker. They may be a violent organization—at least we've heard they're preaching violence."

"What do you think about them?" a student inquired.

"I haven't yet come into contact with any of them nor have I attended any of their meetings. So out of fairness, I wouldn't want to mislabel them. However, Monday night Julian Bond will be here from Atlanta to speak and I plan to attend."

"Should we attend?" In unison, many wanted to know.

"You must decide that for yourselves," he said in a matter-of-fact tone.

Class ended on a sober note. As Carla left the classroom and walked to her car, darkness covered the campus with a stirring tension filling the air. Daily, student restlessness was becoming more obvious. Discussion in class was opened and students didn't hesitate to express themselves. A few of the graduate students expressed concern about the welfare of their young sons or daughters who were attending State College. The BACC threatened the tranquility of the campus.

What was happening? Carla asked herself. She had a heavy-enough course load, but now this. Maybe it would quiet down. She hoped so. Then, again, was she engaging in wishful thinking or even selfish thinking? Getting along well, she didn't want anything to disturb her relationships with the students.

Arms loaded with books from the evening's class, Carla approached the door to her apartment building. The arrogant little manager hurried to hold the door open for her.

"Good evening, Miss Mancari," he said in a cheery voice, "Working late tonight?"

A surge of honesty aroused her conscience. "No. Attending classes at South Carolina State." She blurted out.

In disbelief, he remained rigid, still clutching the door handle as Carla walked past him to the elevator, pushed the button, with her head held high. He didn't say a word, but stood there frozen in the moment, still holding the door.

Early the next morning, Carla exited the elevator to leave for the downtown employment office. The absurd, pathetic creature came running across the lobby to catch up to her. "Oh, Miss Mancari," he called out in a pleading, distressed voice.

"Yes, what is it?" Carla responded, with an irritable edge.

He approached until only inches separated them. In a whisper, he implored, "Please don't mention your attendance at that school to the other renters."

"Sure. If they don't ask, I won't mention it." It was the least she could do. She wasn't morally superior, not with her past record. She had finally realized that truth couldn't be reversed or put on hold.

Intensely relieved, he sheepishly returned to the sanctuary of his office.

Orangeburg's downtown shopping area was laid out in a circular fashion with perpendicular parking in front of the shops. A charming mini-park with a large gazebo was at the center. Palmetto trees and shady oak trees graced the entire grounds.

Carla had agreed to work a few hours a week in the state employment office while attending during the fall and spring semesters. She would also use the office whenever necessary to tape a counseling session for a class assignment. The South Carolina

State Employment building was located on a side street off the circle.

The entire staff was white, and they weren't pleased that she was attending State College. Carla's attendance was taken as a personal insult; it would be an exercise in futility to explain or justify it to them. Besides, her reasons were beginning to become lost in the emotional upheaval she was experiencing.

Carla was overly conscious of all-white faces around her at the office. With her daily attendance at State, it was strange not to see at least one black face. Surely, she thought, there was at least one qualified minority who could fill a position here. She knew the answer, and yet she wondered.

Most of the employees wouldn't associate with Carla. However, one counselor, Sandra, braved the destain of her fellow employees to befriend Carla. A middle-aged woman with stringy brown hair that just covered her ears, Sandra wore dark framed glasses and spoke in a hushed voice.

One day they had lunch together at a nearby restaurant, a cozy place with small round tables. After the waiter had filled the coffee mugs and taken their order, a flushed Sandra said, "Carla, do you know that you're the topic of daily conversation around the office?"

Without taking her gaze off Sandra, Carla raised her mug for a sip of the hot brew. She wasn't sure what Sandra would say next.

Sandra squirmed a little in her seat. "They all respect your work, but they'll never think of you as white again."

In Carla's memory, the dean's warning flashed in large neon lights. "You'll be a marked woman for the rest of your life." So, there was truth in his warning.

The waiter brought their chicken salads. Poking at a piece of lettuce and blinking sadly, Carla raised her eyes to respond. "Among the blacks, I'm considered white. Among the whites, I'm not considered white. God only knows what it is they consider me. "Sandra," she said, half speaking to herself, "when the heart opens, it only knows one color—and that's called human being." Carla had to live with that thought for now.

Sandra was quick to respond. "Most whites are becoming unsettled about the possibility of racial unrest at the school. Unwanted black militants are in the area."

"Is that what you've heard?" Carla asked. Sandra quickly changed the subject. The luncheon ended on a quiet note.

It was the middle of November. The day had absorbed a rainy downpour and the night air was close to becoming cold. Professor Symbolic, in his usual rambunctious form, shared his theory about the sunbathing habits of whites.

With a wide grin glancing in Carla's direction, he began, "The reason whitey goes to the beach and sun bathes to get a tan is because subconsciously, he's trying to become black. Instant nigger!" He held his glance steady as he asked, "Anyone got a better theory?" Laughter filled the room and all eyes turned toward Carla. Then, he gave them a list of all-black books to read. "Are there any about the whites?" He chuckled in his defiant smugness. He was driving her up a wall, but Carla was grateful she was able to keep a closed mouth.

Abruptly, Professor Symbolic's demeanor changed as he warned, "Be careful. Be ready. Things are heating up. We'll all be needed. This is a time for change and for making a difference."

Pacing the room with flung-out hands, he continued, "Those of you who are teachers, prepare yourselves to be called on by the governor and other officials for information and assistance when trouble comes. You young people should no longer be silent!" He was dead serious. As the tension rose, a sense of foreboding hovered over the entire class. Class was dismissed.

Caught up with the individual relationships and her studies the past months, Carla wasn't fully aware of the implications of the professor's warning. Imagining that the next six months could compete with the previous months was difficult.

Tension and restlessness pervaded all aspects of life on campus. The black power sign flashed everywhere. Unable to comprehend where this was leading, Carla felt caught in the grips of a tangled web of ominous unforeseen events to come.

She believed the dean was the best person with whom she should discuss the disgruntled campus atmosphere. She sat in one of his leather chairs and he sat behind his big mahogany desk. Thoughtfully, he opened the conversation.

"Carla, do you know why the president was reluctant to let you into this institution?"

She shook her head. Carla never had realized that the president of the college had been reluctant to accept her.

"He thought you might be a spotter for some kind of black organization, even the Black Awareness Group."

Astonished, she asked, "Why would he think that? That blows me away."

"Carla, you're the first full-time white woman student to attend the college. The president asked me if I wanted to accept you, and when I said yes, he reared back in his chair with a big cigar between his teeth and laughingly replied, 'All right, Doc, she's your baby.'"

They both chuckled and then the dean clasped his hands on the desk top and leaned toward her. His expression was one of deliberate concern.

"Carla, you know about the Black Awareness Group?"

"Yes, I've heard of it."

"Well, great consideration was given whether to allow them on the campus. We already have an active chapter of the NAACP. The faculty decided it's better to allow the Black Awareness Group to organize on the campus so controls could be placed on their meetings. They can use college facilities, but no publicity is to be given to them and a question-and-answer period is to be allowed after each guest speaker's presentation."

His dark circled eyes held a hint of danger. He unclasped his hands and placed his palms down on the desk as though the pressure applied on the desk would steady his universe.

He added, "These groups thrive on publicity, but with the wit and intelligence of the faculty pitched at them, they should fail if their motives aren't in the best interests of the students."

"Dean, how do you think the students will respond to this group?"

"I can't be sure. Their voices are getting louder with every passing day, and we're starting to hear the noise that's being made on the streets all across the nation." He chewed at his lower lip, his jaw muscles tightening. "Reason may not prevail. Tension and emotions are running high."

"Yes, sir. I'm beginning to feel it myself," Carla reluctantly admitted.

He relaxed his hands, cupped them, squared his shoulders and spoke in a caring but urgent voice. "Listen to me carefully, Carla. If any one of them should lay a hand on you—and this could happen off campus as well—you just say to the one who would lay a hand on you that you're 'soul, too.' Got that? 'Soul, too.' It may save your life."

Carla was perplexed. She thought the dean was referring to soul music. She needed to be sure. Totally ignorant, she questioned him. "What does that mean?"

"It means you're a soul sister and that you have Negro blood in you, that you're one of us. It's actually a secret password among the black brothers and sisters."

"It's very kind of you to share that with me."

His mouth softened, and gently he said, "Carla, the time is coming when we all must show concern for each other, no matter what the race or individual differences. People of all races must learn to live together in harmony and concern for each other."

"Yes, dean, I agree."

Thanking the dean for taking the time to see her and for the act of kindness he expressed for her personal safety, Carla left his office. She felt no fear. None. Deeply touched by such a warm and caring individual, she drove off campus with renewed determination to complete her mission here. Now, she wouldn't want to disappoint the dean.

The fall evenings were becoming much cooler. With Daylight Savings Time long over, darkness arrived early. The campus nights held a pervasive deceptive calm.

Carla headed for her evening class. The once-quiet campus was disturbed by the angry young black voices proselytizing their cause.

Because they were engrossed in their own agenda, Carla passed unnoticed. She was left with a sense of anticipation and dread for the trouble that would lie ahead.

10

Cupid's Poor Timing

Strangers with placards disrupted the lull between the change of seasons, from fall to winter. In the final weeks of the fall semester, militant voices captured the ear of many of the student body who stopped to listen.

Most of Carla's time was spent completing projects and working with the study group. And she still was working part-time at the employment office.

As Carla walked to her evening class, Lil joined her for a few minutes. Lil wasn't her usual low-keyed self. She seemed in a highly agitated state.

"Have you heard, have you heard there—there may be a protest march downtown?" Lil stammered.

"No, when is it planned?"

"Not sure yet, Smitty was passing the word. Cleveland Sellers was trying to put it together."

"Ah, yes, I've heard of Cleveland Sellers. Lil, please be careful if you decide to participate."

Their pace slowed a little. There was a pause. Lil calmed and said, "Carla, our study sessions are helping me a lot."

"They're helping me a lot too, Lil."

As Lil moved on to her class, Carla watched how quickly she vanished. The intensity in Lil's voice when she spoke about the protest left Carla with the daunting feeling that Lil was actually telling Carla to be careful.

At times, Smitty joined them during lunch at the cafeteria. Carla was impressed with his persistent dedication to the "cause." He was so young, and, like so many young blacks, he was running out of patience with the local white establishment. She wondered how downtown Orangeburg would receive a protest march. The thought disturbed her, but she understood the students' pent-up frustrations with the local business people.

Carla smiled when she thought of Lil's sweetness. Lil was right about the study group. But for Carla, it was more than helping her with class assignments, it helped her to understand her classmates. It was the study group that brought her into closer contact with other students. The group had grown to seven and it was as close to socializing with them that she came. They'd become comfortable with each other. James was a delight and made her feel like she belonged. Keenly aware she lived in two different, conflicting worlds, Carla moved freely from one world to the other, but for James and his friends it wasn't the same. It was entirely different. They endured problems she'd never thought about.

Carla never worried about going into any restaurant and being refused service. She never worried about living where she pleased. She never worried about being accepted in a good school if she had been academically qualified. The list went on and on. All the things she'd taken for granted, the blacks were denied, because of the color of their skin and a few myths.

In the study group and elsewhere on the campus, the students relaxed and were themselves. They could go to any building on campus, the door was open to them. But when they left the campus, they faced problems of which she never had been aware before attending State College.

She couldn't even fathom what difficulties her white world had helped to create for another race. The mind buttons that they constantly pushed to just survive!

She recorded, "I couldn't handle it, and I believe there aren't many, if any, whites who could. I condemn no one. I'm as guilty as most. I'm sure long before a white man even thought about passing laws against discrimination, God had already done so."

James was waiting just outside of the classroom. He greeted her. They exchanged class notes and hurried to their seats.

Despite the prevailing apprehensive mood, the two-hour class time went well. The students hurriedly filed out the classroom and to their cars. The past weeks, filled with the many class assignments, the study group and papers, had left Carla bone-tired. She wasn't as quick to exit.

After putting on her winter coat, she loaded her arms with her books. She exited the classroom with Professor Good, a man she respected as a superior being of excellent character. As they approached the two flights of descending stairs, Professor Good cupped his left hand beneath her right elbow. Slipping into a racist mental trap, immediately she thought, why was he touching me?

Half-way down the flight of stairs, her brain thawed and she realized he was helping her down the stairs, because her arms were full. There was nothing sinister about it. God, she thought, how deep-seated was her own prejudice rooted and how easily it sprung forth. She was ashamed.

They continued their descent. Professor Good remarked, "It was a beautiful day for playing golf."

"Do you play?" Carla asked, in an upbeat tone.

"Whenever I have the time." He took each step with deliberation, being careful Carla maintained her balance.

Carla stopped her decent for a moment and asked, "Oh, do you play at the local country club?"

There was a deafening pause. Then, in a soft voice he answered, "No, Carla, I don't." He cast his eyes downward and continued to support her.

Insensitive, Carla pursued, "Why not? I hear it has a fine course."

Silence ensued. Once they were on the street level, Professor Good looked away from her gaze toward the lighted buildings of the campus and soulfully said, "It's for whites only. I'm not allowed to play there."

She was aware her inconsiderate ignorance had caused him discomfort. Well-educated, well-dressed, a kind individual who was ostracized because he had a darker shade of skin than a preselected group. Who was possibly any better than this dear person?

She wasn't sure which was worse: The cringe at the top of the stairs or slap she inflicted in his heart at the bottom. Professor Good was the last person she wanted to hurt. She would never forget the quiet pain in this beautiful person's eyes and voice as he said, "It's for whites only." Carla was learning in and out of the classroom.

Professor Sorry, however, still managed to get a reaction out of Carla. "Blacks lack the opportunity to become educated. Government programs are not available to help him catch up nor any community interest in him," he said.

"That's just not so," she countered, and continued uninvited, "There's the STEP program and the Youth Opportunity Centers, which were created for the sole purpose of evaluating disadvantaged youth for training and reeducation."

Professor Sorry's silence, she believed, confirmed the truth of what she said. His moaning and groaning about the unfairness of life wasn't the answer. Self-pity was never an answer. Carla believed it was a terrible disservice.

His silence didn't last long. He uttered another one of his "feel sorry for blacks" sentiments. He concluded and, without looking directly at Carla, he invited a response.

"Yes, Carla?" he said. She had been had. She had taken the bait. She needed to learn to keep her big mouth shut. He knew better than she what the real opportunities were and were not.

Attaining a sense of harmonious balance, Carla's studies and relationships at school were progressing well and, for the first time, she felt well-grounded. But when least expected, life has a strange way of shooting arrows in one's direction.

"Carla, are you busy?" The phone call carried the hushed voice of her friend." I'm preparing the last of the semester's term papers before the Christmas holidays. But I'm never too busy for you, Mary T. What's up?"

"Well, you know I've been looking to trade in my old car."

"Sure. Any luck?"

"Not around here. I haven't been able to get a good trade. How about going to the local auto dealer in Orangeburg tomorrow morning to see what kind of trade they might give me?"

"Without your car?" Carla said in amusement.

"Yes. Just get an idea and then I'll ride up there and talk to them myself. Would you do that for me?"

Carla promised, "Okay, I'll do it."

Only Mary T would've come up with the idea of having someone negotiate a trade without a car. Hanging up, Carla chuckled, "Oh, that Mary T. What will she think of next?"

The middle of December brush-painted the downtown's greenery in shades of brown. A sunny cold promised a white Christmas. The shopping district was bustling with Christmas shoppers.

Locating a parking space near the car dealership, Carla walked into the showroom. An eight-foot Christmas tree with its wide decorated branches stood in the far right corner, white garlands were looped throughout the room, large white snowflakes hung from the ceiling, and the song *Jingle Bells* cheered the air. Four shiny new cars garlanded in gigantic red ribbons graced the floor, several ardent admirers paying them homage.

Carla stood with hands tucked into her winter coat, momentarily caught up in the magical scene.

"Hello, I'm Stan, the sales manager. May I help you?"

Startled, Carla dazedly peered through the haze of a distant Christmas memory. A remarkably good-looking man came into her focus. Dark hair touched with gray at the sideburns, black velvet lashes surrounded sparkling blue eyes. He was tall, well-proportioned. An incredible smile displayed a set of perfectly straight white teeth.

He slightly tilted his head, not sure if she had heard him. She had. She liked the sound of his voice and the perfect mouth.

"Hi, I'm Carla," she managed to introduce herself as she extended her hand. She fell in love instantly.

He too had been stung. Standing there in the middle of the showroom floor, as though they were the only two people in God's creation, he told her about himself. A recent widower with three children—all girls, aged eighteen, sixteen, and three. He drew pictures from his wallet to show a beautiful family. He was especially proud of his three-year-old, whom he called, "my baby," an appealing youngster with fine chestnut brown hair, beautiful large dark brown eyes set in a pretty round face.

His personal questions confirmed he too had been affected—he was also interested.

"Do you live in Orangeburg?

"Yes."

"Where do you work?"

"South Carolina Employment Office."

"Are you married?"

"No."

They were soon past the initial stage of getting acquainted. Carla reminded herself the last thing she needed at this stage in her life was another emotional complication. She had to get out of there, and fast. Making a flimsy excuse, Carla rushed out the door.

Once back in the safety of her apartment, the memory of the warmth of his handshake sent pulsating chills through her mind. He had represented everything she ever wanted in a man. He was too good to be true. It would be such an easy, delicious fall to take.

Carla's practical side insisted she didn't have time for this. She had a term paper to finish and another semester to complete. Be practical, bury yourself in your studies, stay away. But even as she argued with herself, she knew the cause was lost.

Two days later, Mary T and Carla were on their way to the dealer. Carla secretly hoped Stan wouldn't be there. The heart connection had been made. Could it be broken?

The moment they turned into the driveway, she heard, "Hi, Carla! Nice to see you again." Her heart beat so that she checked to see if it was about to burst through her chest.

"Hello, Stan." She replied, avoiding those heavenly blue eyes that reflected the sun's rays. "Stan, this is my friend, Mary Thompson."

They exited the car and were guided to Stan's modest office. Stan offered Mary T a chair beside his desk and Carla sat on a molded chair a few feet away. Stan took his seat and he and Mary T discussed a car trade. Carla was finding it difficult to follow the conversation. All she heard was the sound of a pounding heart—hers.

Carla was taken by his strong jawline and the longest dark lashes she'd ever seen. Impressed with his gentle interaction with Mary T, Carla drifted off momentarily. Recalling his warm handshake, she drew him to her, his warm hands with slender fingers caressed her throat. She held him close and tilted her head upwards to meet his waiting perfect lips. The moment was shattered as Stan rose to test-drive Mary T's car.

Flushed with the dizziness of this man's presence, Carla wondered if it were noticeable. Couldn't everyone see what was happening to her? No. Fortunately, Mary T was focused on acquiring her new toy. Their chatter while they awaited Stan's return was about the car she wanted. Stan returned, and he and Mary T discussed the trade. Few words were exchanged between Stan and Carla. The entire transaction was handled in a professional manner.

Shortly, a deal was struck. With the financial arrangements settled, Mary T and Carla drove away in a brand-new car. Knowing he was watching, Carla controlled the urge to turn and wave goodbye. She was hoping that he hadn't seriously caught whatever it was that she had.

Mary T was ecstatic about her new car. After dropping Carla off, she headed for home, eager to show off her flashy new purchase to her friends.

Carla entered the apartment and checked the mirror for signs of what was going on. Why could she still feel his hands on her? Why could she still hear his gentle voice? Why were his illuminating sky-blue eyes still looking at her?

She thought briefly about her steady gentleman friend, Matt, whom she continued to see as often as possible when she was in Charleston. She was comfortable with him and believed they would marry one day. However, other priorities in her life always seemed to arise. But this man, this man aroused feelings in her she never knew existed.

Fortunately, the school's demands on her time and energy for the next few days didn't allow Carla to delve into the deepest places of her heart. She was relieved to place Stan on hold. The entire notion of his possibility now seemed remote. It was near the end of the semester. She was looking forward to a well-deserved two-week Christmas break.

The final days of the fall semester were over. One last semester was on the horizon. Carla hurried from the third story class building toward her already packed car, when she heard James calling,

"Carla, Carla wait for me."

"Hi, James. Did you get the grades you wanted?"

"Sure did. My dad will be very happy." They both shared a laugh.

"Carla, do you have access to a copying machine?"

"Yes, I do. Do you need something copied?"

"No," a pensive James responded.

Perplexed by his answer, Carla noticed that James appeared distant, almost secretive. As they walked together the few blocks to her car, she wondered what was up. They talked about the called-off protest march against the bowling lanes. The Christmas break might give tempers time to cool. Could this be what's bothering him? Unlocking the driver's door, and opening it wide, Carla tossed her books on the seat. Getting in, she looked up at James, and asked, "What is it? Is anything wrong?"

"I've got it in my hand. I've got it in my hand. Look what I've found," announced an excited James. He quickly walked to the passenger side and got in.

"What do you have? What is it?" Curiosity was getting the best of Carla. His handsome dark face tensed as he handed her a paper folded in two.

"It's a copy," nervously, he informed her. "A copy of the comprehensive examination coming up at the end of next semester. Carla, you can make a copy for yourself, but guard it well." It was the final exam, written and oral, that covered the entire course study for a master's degree.

"James, I don't want the test. It's very thoughtful of you to share it with me and I do appreciate it, but I'll be all right. And you don't need it either. It's too risky. If you need help next semester with the comprehensive, we can study together for the exam." Carla didn't wish to hurt her young friend and hoped that he would see that.

Breathing a long, deep sigh, James was clearly relieved. He really sweated the dreaded comprehensive exam.

"Thanks, Carla, I was hoping we could study together for it." Crumpling the paper in his hand, he frowned and said, "It's not a good idea for me to have this around anyway. Be holy hell if my dad finds out or I get caught."

"Go home, James, and enjoy the Christmas holidays. Don't you worry about it. We'll do fine next semester. I promise."

"Merry Christmas, Carla." Leaving the car, James happily whistled a tune, his old self returned to good cheer.

As Carla drove off campus, she noticed that the grassy slopes on either side of the car had taken on a faded brownish look from the winter's chill. Headed south the interstate to Charleston, Carla's thoughts were still with James and his thinking enough of her to share his precious acquisition. Beyond the right or wrong of it was the simple fact that he wanted to help her, a white person. Moreover, he trusted her. She knew that it was trust that held relationships together. It was trust that would dispel the delusions that exist between the races. His consideration of her made her feel pretty darn good. She liked the feeling.

In Charleston for a two-week break, Carla relaxed from the highly exhilarated pace of the past six months. She wasn't expecting it to ease up any time soon. The time spent with Mary T, Matt and her friends allowed her to slip back into her white world where very little emotional energy was spent. There were no challenges, no constant tugging at her heart. It was a nice change, until—-

"Hello, Carla. How does Mary T like her new car?" Stan's voice on the other end of the phone jolted Carla's complacency. It really had happened. He did exist and was again tugging at her heart strings.

"She loves it," Carla's breathless voice responded.

"Well, you know if she has any problems with it, just let me know."

"I'm sure she will. Thanks for checking on it, Stan."

There was a long pause. It was what he wasn't saying that told her he called to talk with her.

Here it was. "Carla, when will you be back in Orangeburg?"

"In about a week." Carla had abandoned any thought of being evasive.

"May I see you when you return?" Stan's voice had a little shyness in it.

"Stan, why don't you give me a call in a couple of weeks?" That would give her time to collect her thoughts and heart. What she would do with them once collected, she had no idea.

"Thanks, I will," he said in a definite manner. "You have a happy New Year and say hi to Mary T for me."

It became a difficult New Year celebration. Carla waited in anticipation of getting back to Orangeburg. The entire scene at school that held the threat of unrest and protest quickly faded from her mental screen. Her thoughts were embracing the man who would be calling her soon. In her heart, there would be no unnecessary detours, a place had already been prepared for him.

She didn't discuss her latest inner turmoil with her dear friend Mary T. She felt Mary T would only worry that this wasn't the best time to begin a new relationship.

Carla also couldn't explain what was going on with her to Matt. He attributed her haste to get back to Orangeburg to her wanting to complete her last semester. He was eager for her to return home permanently, so they could get on with a normal life. Carla was well past that possibility.

11

A Collision Course

As the January 1968 spring semester approached, President Johnson's build up of over 500,000 American troops in Vietnam caused political divisiveness and grave misgivings among the American people.

The nation had already experienced three "long hot summers" of racial violence and riots—bloody killings, beatings and arrests. In the process, the North and South each had its share of looting, burning and firing upon police.

Faced with the carrying out of Federal anti-segregation court decisions and civil rights' laws, Alabama's governor, George C. Wallace, vowed to maintain the status quo.

However, South Carolina managed to remain racially peaceful. It was a delicate peace that lulled the state into a complacency with a no-nonsense philosophy enforced by a show of force. State officials believed they could forcefully preserve the state's national tranquil racial image from being tarnished by "outsiders." Governor Robert E. McNair resolved to use force if violence erupted. At a press conference, he said, "In dealing with a riot, the only way you can control it is to bring in maximum police power and immediately to isolate, control, and contain. Otherwise, you will have Detroits and Newarks."[3]

---

[3]Jack Bass and Jack Nelson, *The Orangeburg Massacre* (Macon GA: Mercer University Press, 1984) 89.

Dr. Martin Luther King, Jr. made plans for his Poor People's March. A white backlash was manifesting as King's nonviolent movement became more violent under the influence of the "Black Power" slogan of Stokely Carmichael's Student Nonviolent Coordinating Committee. The patience of black students in the North and South was transforming into a growing anger for justice "now."

The students at South Carolina State were trying to work with the local city council to bring about a peaceful solution to the discrimination against the students within the community. By January, 1968, they hadn't met with success. Orangeburg was fast becoming fertile ground for racial turmoil.

It was a cold, damp morning when Carla arrived back on campus for the spring semester. A cold that contained a sweeping chill with a lethal promise. The bold white letters, STATE COLLEGE on the slopes surrounding the entrance served to remind Carla that she was back for her third and final semester. The park, the tennis court, and White Hall were all familiar markers now. As she drove onto the campus, there were no invisible black bars, no bars to clang shut. But there were signs of possible trouble everywhere. Militants recruited among small groups of students and Black Awareness literature passed freely among them. The air of anxiety that covered the campus made it different.

Still somewhat exhausted from the previous semester, Carla's hope was to get through the semester without having to wage any racial battles. An incident-free semester would be a welcome change. Get this semester behind her and she was home free—finished. That was her fervent wish.

She drove through the first intersection and parked the car near the gym for her final registration. She buttoned her winter coat and stooped to retrieve the necessary registration materials from the seat. Mindful of the previous registrations, she began the trek toward the heavy, wooden gym door.

Carla cautiously entered the gym. She was engulfed by the familiar sea of black. This time, there were heartfelt smiles and students greeted her. Like a Sunday-morning church social, she was a welcome member of the congregation. Intensely relieved, she moved forward, without trepidation.

Caressing the moment, she took her place in a long black line. She chatted with those around her and shared their good nature. Getting four class cards stamped and her tuition bill paid, with "byes and "see you laters," Carla was on her way to the bookstore.

To Carla's delight, it was also filled with familiar faces. Taking her place in line behind Brenda, they exchanged their doings over the holiday. Both had been disappointed at not having the white Christmas that weather reports had promised.

Ted, Mark and Hal joined the line. Beaming brightly like a night light in a snow storm, James and Clayton waved without restraint from across the room, and Arnie smiled excitedly as he joined James in greeting their library study mate.

The clerk greeted her with a warm, "Hello and may I help you?" It was the first time a visit to the bookstore had involved Carla's speaking, and she relished the good cheer. Clutching her books, waving and smiling a goodbye to those around, she climbed the narrow stairs. It was a weightless ascension. Lightness and joy penetrated every pore.

The cold, damp weather couldn't dampen Carla's spirits. It took three tries, but she finally had gotten it right. It made her think she just might have that much-wanted trouble-free semester after all.

Tugging at the woolen scarf tossed around her neck, Carla hastened her pace to the car. Seeing protesters, black militants, jolted her back to the reality of the changes that were taking place on campus, in Orangeburg and the nation. Her attention was diverted by the hope that if she were lucky, she wouldn't have Professor Symbolic this semester. That wouldn't only make her day, it would make her entire semester. She drove off campus, and in a few blocks she was back in the warmth of her apartment.

Getting rid of her coat, Carla stacked her newly purchased textbooks on the table. Sitting down, she reviewed the registration materials. She wasn't yet sure who her professors were this semester. Part of the joy of the day dissipated as she was reminded this was the semester for the big one, statistics. It was finally here.

The dean was good enough to allow her to take it in the last semester. It all seemed so long ago—that first visit with the dean. Who could have foreseen the coming events—the Black Awareness Group forming on campus and the militant meetings?

The insistent ringing of the phone interrupted her musings. She was hesitant to answer it because as she reached for the receiver, she knew who it was by the bolt of lightning surging through her heart. Only one individual could do that with the ring of a phone. All her internal warning systems were operational. However, with sheer determination, she was able to override the systems and move into an unknown place within her heart.

"Hi, Carla. It's Stan. Welcome back to Orangeburg," he cheerfully greeted her.

It was no surprise to her. "Hi, Stan," she said with a heady feeling of dizziness.

He immediately announced his intentions. "How would you like to have lunch with me this afternoon?"

"Yes" was the only word in her vocabulary.

"I can meet you downtown at the Sparrow restaurant in an hour," Stan responded.

Within seconds after hanging up, Carla was terror struck with the thought, how would he react to her attending a black college? Orangeburg was such a closed-minded segregationist town. She wasn't sure how to handle it. But something would come, it always did.

It was a short drive to the restaurant Stan had chosen. Parking her car, she walked to the door, took a long deep breath and entered the restaurant. The heightened anticipation of seeing this man again tingled every nerve ending in her body.

He was there, just a short distance from her. His sparkling white teeth were like a beacon in a turbulent storm. His presence exuded masculine charm that excluded all others around him. In seconds he was at her side, helping her off with her coat and placing it on a nearby hanger. She looked lovely in her navy-blue skirt that followed the slim contours of her body, the light-blue silk blouse, navy-blue cardigan, and navy walking shoes. He liked what he saw. The two long weeks had been worth the wait. He was enchanted by this dark-haired, dark-eyed beauty he met only three weeks ago.

He guided her through the closely-placed tables to one next to a wall. As he held a chair for her, he said, "Less noisy here."

Sitting, she adjusted the chair, casually looked around, and remarked, "This is a charming place and everyone seems to know one another." The constant flow of chatter lyrically filled the spaces. From across the room, several couples waved at Stan.

Nervous, Carla tried a little small talk. "Most of the diners seem to know you."

"That's because I'm a regular here. I eat here two or three times a week. The food is good," Stan assured her.

"I like the decor. So much greenery and hanging green plants."

"Yes," he informed her, "it's what they're most known for. They're all live plants. It's like a large garden."

The waitress greeted Stan with a friendly acknowledgment and gave them the menus to review. Immediately, Stan knew what he wanted, but asked the waitress to give them a few minutes. He then helped Carla make her choice from the most favorite dishes.

The waitress returned and they placed their order. While they were waiting for their food, Stan talked a little more about himself.

"My father died when I was a young boy. I'm an only child. But have plenty of uncles, aunts, and cousins.

"Carla, you're the first woman I've asked out since my wife's passing." He glanced down at the white table cloth, momentarily absorbed in a painful memory. His long dark lashes curved slightly and a frown etched across his brow. "I lost her to a blood disease last year. She was ill from the time of our last child, Cathy." The thought of his little girl put a tender smile on his handsome face. "My eldest girl is in her last year of high school. She'll be attending college in the fall. The middle girl has two more years of high school."

"I'm sorry, about your wife. It must be a painful memory for you."

"Memories are the burden we must bear. But not all memories are painful," he said, studying her.

Thankfully, the waitress arrived with their orders. Carla wasn't sure how to deal with such a profound loss. For the moment, at least, she had all the stress she could handle. However, she liked the idea that he had children—something she had always wanted.

The waitress placed their food before them, poured coffee and retreated. Between bites of baked flounder, Carla sought to engage Stan in a more general, light conversation. "How long have you been with the car dealership?"

"Twelve years. I started with them right after my discharge from the military." Then he proudly added, "I began as a salesman, got the promotion to sales manager six years ago."

His penetrating blue eyes caused Carla to look away while she searched for anything she could possibly think of to keep the conversation from becoming focused on her. "Do you like the work?" Was the best she could come up with. Her mind was scattered and her pounding heart was making her food difficult to swallow.

He grinned. "I love it. But enough about me. Tell me about yourself." Stan rapidly fired at Carla the question she was trying so hard to avoid. "How long will you be working in Orangeburg? I believe you said you were working for the State Employment Office?"

She was in a real quandary. Still not sure how to handle the answer, she responded with a half truth.

"Yes, I work for the Employment Office." Carla didn't volunteer any more then she had too. She had done this before with the apartment manager and it had worked but, not for long.

"How long will you be in Orangeburg?" Stan repeated. He wanted to know.

"I'll be here through the first week of May," Carla reluctantly answered.

"Carla, would you like more coffee?" That was the first question Carla welcomed and answered without hesitation.

"Yes, please." His square chin with its carved dimple caused Carla to ask herself, why hadn't I noticed that before? His generous black hair combed back had a natural wave. The white in his sideburns lent an air of maturity. She couldn't investigate this delightful man enough.

Stan signaled the waitress to refill their coffee cups. She immediately came forth with a steaming hot pot of coffee. The moment she turned to leave, Stan asked, "Do you like your work?"

The reprieve was short-lived. "Yes, I like it very much."

He didn't have the slightest idea what was going on with her. The only ones in this town who knew were her co-workers in the office and her apartment manager. He wasn't about to tell anyone.

Most whites in Orangeburg wouldn't begin to suspect that a white southern woman would ever consider attending a black college. It was just too incomprehensible.

Carla tried to convince herself Stan needn't know, that it wasn't serious between them. She was playing a head game, while her heart knew better. Her heart knew long before she did just what a dangerous game she was playing.

Stan had an agenda of his own. He reached across the table and lightly touched Carla's resting hand. "Carla, I want to see you again. You know, I only called Mrs. Thompson to ask about the car during the holidays in hopes of talking with you."

Yes, Carla knew. That phone call had her brain in a fever-pitched mode. But the overwhelming emotional tug-of-war that was being waged within her was much more than she had expected. She slowly withdrew her hand from his sensual touch and changed the subject.

Lunch over, Stan helped Carla with her coat and walked her to the car. He inserted the key in the door lock and opened the door. Carla slid onto the seat, closed the door, and started the engine. Stan leaned toward her through the open window. He wasn't about to end it there. He looked at her steadily with those tantalizing blue eyes. His nearness sent her thinking mechanisms into a tizzy.

"Carla, can we go out one evening soon?"

Her rattled brain argued, this wasn't a good idea. You've enough pressure at school juggling two different and conflicting worlds. It was a full-time job in itself. Adding romance to it was like pouring fuel on a blazing fire. He made her feel that way—on fire! So the whole idea was out. It must stop here and now.

"Yes, you may call in a couple of days." She wondered, why am I feeding the very fire that is consuming me?

Stan broadly smiled as he waved her off. All Carla could think was: Damn! Eight months ago this wouldn't have been a problem. What a difference a few months made. A few months and a lot of blacks she never knew before.

Carla returned to the apartment feeling a mixture of boiling elation and guilt. Matt never for one moment crossed her mind or heart. She was on a runaway train and she had no idea where the tracks led. For tonight, at least, she must gather what was left of her thinking abilities and prepare for tomorrow morning's early class. It would be the first day of the spring semester.

Professor Sammy again taught the early-morning class in advanced practical counseling. He greeted Carla warmly.

"Carla, it's good to have you in my class again." He was as black and as brilliant as ever. Still, there was a fringe of amusement about that combination from whatever leftover racial conditioning she had been exposed to.

"Thank you. It's good to be back." She'd come to appreciate this bright, energetic, articulate man's devotion to teaching. She knew now she was capable of learning from this individual no matter what combination existed. It was significant she recognized that.

In the first evening class of the semester, James spied Carla entering the classroom and switched his seat to sit next to her. They chatted before class began. Carla was surprised to see a white student walk through the door. A middle-aged slightly bald man. He looked uncertainly around the room, saw her, and smiled as if greatly relieved. He walked over and introduced himself to her.

"Hi, I'm Paul." He took a seat nearby, and James gleefully filled her in. Paul was a school superintendent or, as James put it, "A school super." James was his mischievous self. As Carla and James were engrossed in making plans to continue their weekly studies together in the library, a thunderous voice shouted over the classroom chatter, "Carla, we're so glad to see you."

It was Norton. A large black hand reached for hers. Carla joyously placed her hand in his. The clasp of their hands and the pleasure in his eyes instantly renewed their friendship. Norton and Crystal were in this class, commuting together from Charleston. They sat as near to Carla as possible. Class began.

In walked the new instructor. A tall, little on the heavy side, sporting a full round face with large lips and large brown eyes. He wore his hair in a round, frizzy style. He was a quiet, soft-spoken pleasant man, who was extremely courteous. He didn't interrupt anyone without a "pardon please." He was full of pleases and thank yous. Carla designated him Professor Polite.

The two hours went by quickly. It was exciting being back among old friends. Norton and Crystal wanted to visit with her after class, but unfortunately, they missed the chance to chat because the hour was late and they had a long drive home to Charleston. Norton promised, "We'll get in a little early before Saturday morning's class and spend some time with you." They exchanged smiles and were gone.

Carla headed for her car. It was a cold, clear dark night. Imbedded in the heavenly darkness were the distant sparks of light. The campus was almost deserted. She drove off campus to the comfort of her apartment where she wasn't looking forward to tomorrow evening's class—statistics.

When it finally was time for the class, Carla was caught totally off guard. It was held in the familiar three story building, but she had the most interesting looking professor thus far. A huge man, with puffy, dark brown cheeks, a well-trimmed beard and mustache. With his great sense of humor and a hearty laugh, he put a little fun into the class discussions. Carla liked him. He reminded her of a black Santa Claus without the long whiskers and red cheeks.

"Statistics is, for many students, a very dry subject. Well, rest assured, I plan to pour some water on it," he laughed. And the entire classroom laughed with him. If he could get Carla to like statistics, he was Santa Claus! And, of course, she called him Professor Santa Claus.

Another white student in this class also worked for the local school system, a middle-aged man of average height, with blond hair, blue eyes. Carla smiled from across the room. She didn't feel a need to go running over to sit next to him. Had either of them been on campus last summer, she probably would've developed a friendship, a bond.

It felt good to see other white students taking advantage of the education that was offered at State—good for the white and the black students. She only wished that one of them had been in Professor Symbolic's class last semester. Perhaps he would've stuck more to the subject matter.

The best part about this class was that Carla felt relaxed, not a bit under the pressure she felt sure a statistics class would cause. It was a pleasant surprise after dreading it for months. Carla left this evening's class thinking for the first time that she could do it. Professor Santa Claus said, "You can all do it."

Carla had barely opened her apartment door when the phone rang. She was, of course, expecting this call. Relief welled up in her when she answered and heard, "Hi, Carla, it's Stan." She knew that by the ring of the phone. How could a ring of a phone tell her?

"How's your stay in Orangeburg going?" he politely asked.

"Oh, fine, everything is just fine." Enough about her. She wanted more of him.

"Carla, have you ever been to a stock car race?" He was hoping to entertain her in an unusual way.

"No, Stan, I haven't. Never had the opportunity to go to one." It was good to be able to give a full and honest answer to his question.

"Well, you do now. How about tomorrow night? We have a stock car race speedway on the outskirts of Orangeburg." He was pleased with himself. He would be able to share an interest with her.

They agreed on a time for Stan to pick her up at the apartment. It was their first evening date and Carla had all of the butterflies of a teenager anticipating her first date.

Arriving on time, Stan knocked softly on the apartment door. Carla, dressed for the out-door sports event, opened the door, and welcomed him into her apartment—and her life.

The drive to the race track was a pleasant one. They mostly talked about the car business and how well it was doing. Stan bragged about some of the sales tricks of the trade. Once they arrived at the race track, they sat on one of the wooden benches, joining a crowd of about seventy-five people enjoying the races.

Cars swiftly circled the small dirt speedway, not all of the beat-up cars made it around. The near-misses and collisions caused a roar of excitement from the attentive crowd. Two of Stan's male friends joined them on their wooden bench. Most of the conversation from this point on was all about the stock cars, how they were prepared, repaired, and who were the best drivers. Stan was in his element.

Races over, Stan and Carla said good night to Stan's friends, and stopped at a near-by coffee shop for a cup of coffee before ending the evening. Still high on the evening's event, Stan informed Carla, "I own one of the cars you saw in the race tonight and I sponsor it in local races here and around South Carolina. I bet you could guess which one?" That didn't surprise Carla. His interest and love of the sport was obvious.

"The one that constantly brought you to your feet."

"Right," he laughed.

Stan also wanted Carla to know how he felt about the racial issue. He realized her work involved minorities. He wanted no misunderstanding. "Carla, I know you work with blacks in your job, counseling them. So I think you should know where I stand on the race issue." Here it comes. His handsome features were cast in a shadow of darkness, and his striking blue eyes struck horror sinking feelings in her. "I'm a segregationist, and I'm committed to fighting integration of any kind."

He was confident Carla agreed with him and they could get on with their courtship unencumbered. He knew where he was going with this relationship and he wanted to get there as quickly as possible.

For Carla, it was a dilemma of the worst kind. Yes, she did suspect this would be his racial attitude. But as long as he hadn't spoken those words aloud, she had a thread of hope. Now, the thread no longer existed. She was a little taken back by his candor. She could tell him the truth about her own situation, or avoid the truth as she once did with the apartment manager.

It was not very long ago that she realized the truth could not be put on hold. As she tore her eyes from him, her insides wrenched in a gloomy atmosphere. Carla attempted to open her mouth, but her courage silently came tumbling down. She stirred her coffee, smiled faintly, and opted once more for avoidance. She was the coward. Deciding not to reveal her attendance at State College, she returned to the subject of stock car racing, asking every conceivable question she could conjure up.

In a manly shift, Stan's mood instantly lightened up and his old charm glowed. He had taken the attitude he could definitely impress Carla on the subject. The evening ended at her door with a tender kiss and the promise he would call her soon again.

Stan evaluated his courting strategy and believed he was doing exceptionally well. For him, the evening went very well. He was pleased with his dark-haired beauty. And now that Carla knew his racial views, he was ready to speed up the relationship. He had a plan to disarm and pull her even faster and deeper into *his* universal orbit.

For Carla, the evening plunged her into deeper doubt and confusion. Her brain reeled wildly. How could she possibly continue to see this man? She had a preview—a private glimpse—at the dark side of Stan. It was a place she didn't want to go.

Two days later, the first snowfall of the season canceled the opening session of her first Saturday morning class. The chance to return to Charleston for the weekend was welcomed. She felt an urgent need to sort things out in her head, and heart, about Stan.

Carla told Mary T that she was seeing Stan. When she explained his racial attitude, Mary T was quiet and left Carla with the impression of we'll just wait and see. Mary T wanted to believe that there was nothing there to be concerned about. However, there also was Matt to consider. He, too, must be told. And the telling wasn't an easy task. However, Matt wasn't totally unaware that something had taken place these past few weeks. The change in Carla that it had wrought was obvious to him. He was wise enough to know that she was on a collision course. The weekend hadn't restored the inner calm for that which she so desperately hungered.

12

Transformation

The grassy slopes were the only areas left with telltale signs from last week's blanket of snow. The streets were cleared of ice, but the steam of violence was rising. As Carla drove onto the campus, she was given a black power closed-fist greeting.

Back in her apartment, a familiar phone ring disrupted Carla's studies for an evening class. She both wanted to hear from Stan and feared the consequences of moving in his direction. A small part of her had hoped the weekend dulled his interest in her, a very small part of her.

Dragging her mind away from her studies, she answered the phone. A pleading Stan requested, "Carla, may I come over?" There was little time before her class. She needed to keep her mind clear. Just talking with him on the phone clogged her thinking process. Seeing him put it in deep freeze. Not a good idea.

"Stan, I have to be somewhere by 7:00 PM." The hope was that this would at least discourage him for a time. Then perhaps she could find her way back to a common-sense balance that was necessary to withstand an onslaught of an emotional tidal wave.

"Carla, I've someone for you to meet." He was insistent. "We won't be long." Who could he possibly want her to meet? No way she could do this now. But he had a plea of urgency in his voice. And, she was longing to see this man who kept her in an oddly uncomfortably romantic stupor.

In a no-nonsense compromise, Carla consented. "Okay, Stan, but just for an hour." Having put a time limit on his visit, she felt in control. School was still her priority. She wished she were strong enough to tell him where it was she had to be at seven.

At 5:30 PM, there was a tapping at the door. Swallowing hard and believing she had her emotions safely armored, Carla opened the door. There stood Stan and a gorgeous child with soft shiny chestnut-brown hair flowing to her little shoulders. She had a round beautiful face with big dark-brown eyes and soft milky-white skin, exactly like the picture Stan had showed her. Carla's defenses crumbled.

Swinging the door wide open, Carla invited them to step in. "This is Cathy," a beaming Stan introduced her. "Cathy is only three, but I've told her about you and she wanted to meet you." What could he possibly have told this beautiful child?

An adorable, lovable trusting child, she was a little shy at first, but a real sweetheart. Soon she was sitting on Carla's lap and telling her all the names of her favorite dolls. A relaxed Stan sat across from them. He was positively glowing with pride as he enjoyed the interaction between Carla and his "baby."

Stan knew Carla's heart better now than she did before. He'd always been sure of her from the first time he saw her standing in the auto showroom. He loved the way she tilted her head, smiled and greeted him. She filled him with light then, as she did now.

They stayed the full hour and Carla found herself not wanting them to leave. Cathy gave Carla a big goodbye hug and Stan assured Carla that she would be seeing more of them very soon.

It wasn't fair. Cathy would be easy to love, easy to care for. What chance now did Carla have? The cards were stacked against her. The man of her dreams and now, a darling little one, a baby she would die for. Carla was hooked. She was in over her head.

Stan and Carla were opposites. Yet the emotional and physical pull was overwhelming. She had waited all her life for him. He represented the promise of a love she had always wanted. Chills were running up and down her spine; they also ran sideways. Whenever Stan looked at her, it aroused a breathless heat. It warmed her from head to toe and back again. Oh, how she wanted more of him! She could hardly wait to see him again.

She would see him again in two days, Sunday evening. Stan would be picking her up for dinner and a movie. She found that movies were one of Stan's favorite pastimes.

Carla quickly came to the conclusion that a relationship couldn't be based on deceit. Besides, she felt she would break out in a cold sweat every time he talked about her work. She could no longer handle the tension. It was time, she reasoned, she would tell him. In two days, she would know how he reacted to the truth.

The two-day wait was difficult for Carla. She was both anxious to get the truth behind her and in dread of a confrontation with Stan. Carla reminded herself that for the next two days she must stay focused on her studies. She managed to get through the evening class. The following day she met James in the library with two other students from their class, Brenda and Clayton.

James gave Carla the news, "Lil isn't returning this semester." James was noticeably disappointed. James and Lil were good friends.

"Will she be back for the fall term?" Carla inquired.

Brenda joined the conversation. "I think so. Some financial problems, I think."

"I'm sorry to hear that. Lil's a bright student. She was determined to finish her education, and I believe she will."

They settled in and began to review their class assignments. Clayton couldn't keep his mind on his studies. Carla didn't know him well, but she had never seen him with so much nervous energy.

Suddenly, Clayton excused himself and walked quickly out of the library. "Is he all right?" Carla asked.

Brenda replied, "He's okay. He just has a meeting to attend." His abrupt departure reflected the unrest. Many meetings were being held on campus lately. The Orangeburg bowling alley's whites-only policy was causing the threat of violence, especially among the younger students. Violence was fast becoming a possibility. The growing threat of violence mirrored Carla's inner turmoil.

Finally, the first session of the Saturday morning class was held. The thought of what tomorrow evening with Stan might bring was ever on Carla's mind. However, she had been looking forward to seeing Norton and Crystal again. She arrived on campus early to attend the class. Many off-campus working graduate students attended this class.

As Carla was getting out of her car, another car pulled up directly behind her. The two occupants waved for her to come join them. It was Norton and Crystal.

Norton called out, "Come on. Get in. We still have a few minutes before class." He reached over the top of the front seat for the inside back door release, flipped it and pushed the door outward in Carla's direction.

Smiling, Carla slid into the back seat.

"I brought new baby pictures to show you," Norton said proudly. There was an exhilaration in his voice as he marveled, "Carla, just look how much he's grown."

"Yes, he's growing fast. He's a good size for his age," Carla agreed.

Crystal laughed, "He should be! Look at his big daddy."

"Crystal, how are you doing with the new teaching job?" Carla inquired.

"I'm enjoying it."

"How did your last semester go?" Crystal wanted to know.

Carla smiled. With a matter-of-fact response, she said, "It had its moments."

Norton laughed. "Yeah, I'll bet it did."

Crystal noted, "It's time for class."

"Right," Norton replied, gathering up the baby pictures and tucking them into the glove compartment. "We'll talk again, Carla," Norton assured as they exited the car.

Walking into the classroom, Carla saw three familiar faces from the summer session. They were happy to see her and immediately began to exchange friendly greetings.

Soon there was a rush of students surrounding Carla. They all wanted to greet her and catch up on her school progress. The moment there was a pause, other students came hurrying over to her. While one student talked with Carla, another wanted to tell her something. As they all were vying for her attention, a voice loud and clear shouted, "Carla, girl, you looking good! You put some meat on those bones?"

What a joy it was to look into Thelma's smiling face.

"Thelma!" Carla exclaimed, truly excited to see her. "It's wonderful to see you. Is Marie here?"

Her face grew stern. "No honey, not this semester. Robert convinced her to wait for the next one."

The classroom was soon filled with old friends. Many of the faces Carla recognized from her first semester, the summer session. Most of these students could only attend a Saturday class because they were teaching during the week. Norton and Crystal were the only ones from the summer who were also able to attend an evening class this semester.

Carla took a seat in the center of a black circle. No empty seats around or near her. How different this was for her. No longer did she just see a mass of black faces. The sea of blackness had individual waves in it. They were each recognizable, unique. Black wasn't just black anymore.

For a while now, her perceptions of blacks had started to change. She'd become aware of the differences, but this morning all of Carla's perceptions were heightened. They had gone from the intellectual to the visceral.

Carla had come to recognize that true Christian beliefs and a racist mind were not compatible. The spirit of God flowed through the veins of all His children. The heart that beat within each and everyone was the voice of God. It could not be denied. She could not deny it.

Then, of course, in walked Professor Symbolic. He entered the classroom with his usual swagger and air of smugness. Carla would just have to brace herself for one more "whitey" semester with this pompous ass. But even he couldn't completely dampen her good mood. By now she should be used to him or he used to her. Oh well, she reasoned, it wouldn't be school without him.

She had, after all, been fortunate to have Professor Good and Professor Sammy. They helped to increase her understanding about herself and one's own historical background and gave her a chance to learn to understand other races. Reassessing these past months, she was sure of it. They forced her to dig deep within her own racial pettiness.

Knowing oneself was necessary before one could counsel others. If she didn't understand herself and her motivations, how could she relate to and work with people who were different from her?

What a disjunctive thought that was. She was contemplating the benefits of integration. Never thought she would encourage it. Not in her wildest dreams. No, not her. A transformation, it was a transformation.

Leaving this morning class, she walked on cloud nine. Even the strange young black men on campus who cast their militant looks in her direction didn't penetrate her tranquil mood.

That evening, she recorded, "This morning they were each special in his or her own way. The differences in their shades of color, features, hair texture, size and shapes are individual differences that I had never been so keenly aware of with the Negro.

"Blacks were always just black. 'If you've seen one, you've seen them all.' Another myth bit the dust. Thank God for that. How restricted and narrow my vision must've been. Maybe now I'm seeing with the heart instead of with the mind. It's a complete change from anything else that I have experienced since being on campus—or in my entire life, for that matter.

"I feel I belong—belong here, to this school. It's my college, my campus, my classroom, my friends; just about everything is mine. I have the wonderful feeling of being a whole complete person for the first time in my life—a very special, unique, individual person. And it happened here, on a black campus, among black students.

"I wonder how many others ever come to the conclusion that each individual is different, absolutely unique. I have always said it about other people. However, saying it, or reading about it, isn't the same as experiencing it.

"That's the way the students made me feel in class this morning. And to just think I could've gone all through life and missed this feeling that these students have given to me. It's a wonderful precious gift—a gift of themselves. I feel sorry for those, like myself less than a year ago, who only saw black as black. They are the ones who are the losers—big losers."

Carla didn't get much sleep that night. But it wasn't due to stark naked fear—just the opposite. She was in the grips of sheer bubbly elation. It was the kind of sleep she didn't mind losing. Besides, tomorrow was Sunday, she could sleep late.

That did it. The thought of Sunday and the impending date with Stan brought her tumbling down from cloud nine to a cloud of uncertainty. She was a trapeze artist swinging from bar to bar without a net. If she fell, who would catch her?

13

Devastated

She wanted to collapse in the embrace of his strong masculinity, to let go, to let go of everything, to pretend that this was all there was. But there was more, and she knew it. Stan relaxed his hold and gently kissed her lips. "I've missed you. It seems like an eternity since we were last together," he said.

Stan was eager to be with Carla. For him, the past two days had seemed endless. He discovered he didn't like being away from her for any length of time. He was in love, and he knew it.

The day had been difficult for Carla—vacillating between the joyous residue of Saturday morning and the unbearable thought of facing Stan with the truth. He was moving quickly, far too quickly. Carla steadied herself and withdrew from his embrace.

"It's good to see you again, Stan," she managed to say, turning away from his gaze. To say more might betray the uncertainty gnawing at her insides.

She retrieved a coat for the evening and they left the apartment for an early dinner at the Sparrow. She was glad they were going there. The lush greenery would help lift her spirits.

Stan was in an upbeat mood. His strong jaw relaxed and an intermittent smile intervened as he talked the entire drive to the restaurant. He told her how much the baby enjoyed being with her.

Carla listened with the expectancy of the entire picture of Stan, and the baby being erased from her life's dream. She glanced briefly at Stan. He was a delight to be with when she was in his bright side. It was the dark side of him that had her in an ominous tail spin.

How many weeks ago had she met this man? This man, who now encompassed her present and future plans. What was it? Four—five weeks? How was that possible?

When they arrived at the restaurant, Stan was so into himself, his doings, his plans that he didn't realize Carla had contributed very little to the conversation.

He placed Carla's hand in his as if it were an act he'd performed all his life. He was in such good humor, Carla was doing her best to find ways not to ruin it. Perhaps the truth could wait for another day, another time. But would yesterday's class experience with the students allow any backsliding? Was there a switch she could turn off and on? Was the transformation that had so recently taken place a temporary one?

Tonight, this moment would test its permanency. Courage wasn't what she needed. It was to find that place within her that only yesterday made her truly aware of who and what she really was.

They were barely seated when, in a voice hardly recognizable, Carla confessed, "Stan, I'm not here to work at the employment office. I'm here to attend classes at State College."

It was done. She never intended to hurt him. She could no longer dance around the truth. She had been dancing with the devil. Now, it was time to change. Her new partner would be the truth.

Stan was pale and quiet. He slumped a little, and then said, "Okay. Carla, I want you to meet my two older girls." He appeared distant, not well focused. Carla wasn't sure if he heard her.

"Stan, are you all right?" She asked in a whisper. His usually bright blue eyes had a deadness to them. His mouth clinched, his jaw muscles momentarily flexed nervously.

"Stan, are you sure you want me to meet your girls?" Carla wanted to be sure she heard right.

"Yes, we'll have lunch next week at Vents cafeteria." His dark lashes gave temporary coverage. He was holding up the menu and motioned the waitress to take their order. Carla briefly scanned the menu. What she selected wasn't important. Eating would be difficult, if not impossible.

The waitress collected the menus and left to place their order. Sure that Stan must've misunderstood her, Carla was about to repeat her confession when Stan said, in a deliberate, calm voice, "Carla, do me a favor and don't mention the school to the girls. I'll need time to break it to them myself."

Now resuming his usual erect posture, Stan was able to think more clearly. He was attempting to put together the pieces of his life in a way that could include Carla.

Stan spoke in a soft voice as he reached across the table for her hand. "Carla, I know and love you. The girls will need time to get to know you first, and then I'm sure they'll feel about you as I do."

His touch was sensually warm. Carla struggled to restore and frame her wavering thoughts. She didn't want the continuation of a falsehood. She wanted to change partners for the truth.

Stan insisted that it would be fine. "Carla, I just want the girls to get to know you first. They're still getting over the loss of their mother. Meeting someone new is going to be difficult enough for them, but this other could be devastating."

Carla withdrew her hand from his, tilted her chin slightly, and glared at him with incredulous disbelief. "Stan, is that the way you feel about it, devastated?"

Calmly, in full control, Stan reminded Carla, "You must realize we're all segregationists. We strongly believe in separation, not integration."

She was well aware of the segregationist part. He had been up front with her about it. Perhaps, she thought, she wasn't being entirely fair with him. After all, she did just spring this on him ten minutes ago. It was apparent that Stan, too, needed time to adjust.

Carla let out a sigh of surrender and conceded, "All right, Stan, we'll do it your way for a while."

They ate very little and skipped the movie. A quiet stillness accompanied them on the ride back to Carla's apartment. He had promised to have her back at an early hour. Now he understood why it was necessary. She studied and attended classes. He didn't approve, but for the moment, he was accepting it. They embraced and kissed good night.

The past two days had taken their toll. Although the ups and the downs left her in a fitful exhaustion, she fell asleep more to escape than to rest.

It was a busy week adjusting to two new professors, studying, sharing with the library group, and talking daily on the phone with Stan when she was not seeing him. Saturday's class quickly rolled around. Once again, Professor Symbolic wasn't cutting her any slack.

"Whitey is in for a day of reckoning and his time may very well be now. He will reap what he's sowing and it isn't a very edible harvest. The fruits of whitey's labor are as rotten as his treatment of blacks." His anger this morning was evident.

Instead of encouraging the students to control their emotions, he invited anger. She began to suspect that Professor Symbolic knew more about a planned disruption on the campus than he was admitting.

Carla left his class deciding it was time to discuss her concerns with the dean. She called for an appointment. Detecting an air of disturbance in Carla's voice, the dean's secretary allowed her to come in at once.

The dean, as always, was pleased to see her. Immediately after the exchange of greetings, Carla got right to the reason for visiting on such short notice.

"Dean, I believe Professor Symbolic agitates the class with his talk of militant doom." The dean was shrouded in a cloak of serious thought. However, he didn't see it the same way. He picked his words carefully.

"Carla, I apologize for his remarks, but I do believe that it's only a harmless way to let off steam."

The dean then turned his attention to his concern for her in the statistics class. "I want to hear how you're doing in statistics."

"I'm struggling with it, but I really like Professor Santa Claus. If anyone can teach me to understand statistics, it'll be him."

The dean was pleased to hear it. Not appeased by the dean's response to her concerns about Professor Symbolic's racial remarks, Carla returned to the subject.

"Dean, I'm not convinced. The once-peaceful calm of the campus is slowly unraveling. These kind of racial remarks contribute to the unrest."

The dean studied the face of his most unlikely student for a moment. He fingered a pencil on his desk, then he looked up, the lines across his forehead deepening. He sighed, and said, "Carla, perhaps you're a little too sensitive to the racial remarks. What with the racial tensions within our society being what they are, the classroom is considered a safe place for an otherwise hostile discussion. It probably helps the students and some professors to let off steam. Cooling off here may keep them from boiling over out there."

Silence filled every space in the room. The dean still had Carla's attention as he requested, "Please, give it some thought, will you?"

"Of course, I will. You may very well be right."

She left the dean's office with a reminder to come see him whenever she wished.

Carla felt better after having talked with the dean. He had a way of doing that for her. She reminded herself that both on and off the campus the other students did have a balancing act, blacks were, after all, the ones who were constantly living between two different worlds.

Carla hurried back to the apartment. This was the Saturday afternoon she was to meet Stan's teenage daughters at the downtown cafeteria. It was a rush to shower, and wash away haunted doubts about this meeting, change clothes and drive to the cafeteria. She didn't want to be late.

The events of the day hadn't left her time to collect her thoughts or, for that matter, to give much thought to the seriousness of the path she was about to take. She had successfully numbed herself to any warning signals.

Stan and the girls were seated and waiting for her arrival. Carla glanced at her wristwatch. She was a little late. Stan rose to greet her and introduced his two teenage daughters. With introductions behind them, they collected their food from the cafeteria line. Returning to their table, Carla desperately tried to converse with the older girls. They were polite but remained withdrawn. Perhaps that was a blessing. Beyond small talk there wasn't much she could really talk about. Besides, Carla believed their distant behavior was to be expected under the circumstances.

The baby, Cathy, was all over Carla. They had quickly become good friends. Though he was a little tense, Stan handled the situation well. It was obvious how relieved he was that the initial introductions were over. Fortunately, the ordeal was short. Carla said her goodbyes in the cafeteria parking lot and drove back to the apartment for a long evening of studying.

The evening was interrupted with a phone call from Mary T. Carla related the afternoon's outing with Stan and his daughters. Mary T immediately picked up on the turbulence in Carla's life.

"Carla, please slow down. You could be taking a path that has more twists and turns than you're prepared for," warned Mary T.

Oblivious of all danger hidden in this forbidden love, Carla could only respond.

"I'm lost in him."

"That's all the more reason for you to proceed with caution."

"You're right, of course," she agreed. She returned to her studies, keeping in mind that she was expected to work a few hours at the Orangeburg employment office first thing Monday morning.

Carla's first client was a twenty-two year-old black man who had been recently discharged from the service.

A growing rapport was felt between them. Albert explained, "I'm from a large family and I'm helping my younger sister who's still in high school. I've always wanted to be the first in my family to go to college, but was drafted before I could get in. I want to be an accountant, but my family needs me to earn money, so I'd be content to work for the post office."

Carla was keenly aware of the difference in this counseling session and what they had been like a year ago, before Orangeburg, before Professor Sammy.

It wasn't just a matter of seeing him differently, she perceived him differently. No distance between them, nor any barriers of any kind existed. They weren't relating in black or white, but rather human-to-human.

Carla once thought that she worked well with blacks. She knew now that she had only been working with them indirectly. It was patronizing, not a humanizing experience. In this interview, there was a softness that she'd never experienced before. Carla couldn't do enough for Albert. She wanted genuinely to help this individual in need.

14

Two Worlds Collide

A lethal stillness overshadowed the city. Nothing stirred. It was a city plunged into a deep quiet that hurt the ear and fear crept coldly in. Monday evening, 5 February, Stan and Carla drove back into town after having seen a movie in Columbia, forty miles northwest.

A few hours before, all seemed normal. Driving toward her apartment, they saw deserted streets. It was disconcerting, disturbing, even scary. The entire city seemed abandoned.

"I've never seen the streets like this before. It's a ghost town. It's only 10:30 PM, and it looks as if it's 2:00 AM," Stan remarked in amazement.

"You're right. In fact, 2:00 AM isn't this deserted. It's eerie. It gives me the creeps. It has a real 'twilight zone' feel to it." Carla had never seen anything as this before.

They looked from one side of the street to the other as they drove along. They looked for signs of life. The shops downtown were closed and secured. Most of the houses were dark with shades drawn. They wanted desperately to hear or see something, someone. They detected no movement of any kind. Baffled by the unexpected, Stan shook his head in disbelief and said, "It's not the same town we left a few hours ago, Carla."

Carla was stymied. With a sense of loss and sheer emptiness, she aggressively grasped to make some sense of it. In just a few short hours, the world as she knew it had changed. A hollow silence had replaced it. Her mind stalled in disbelief.

Arriving at the apartment building, Stan parked and they got out of the car. They entered the building, walked through the lobby, stepped into the elevator and rode to the second floor. Still, no sound. No one was around. Stan walked Carla to her apartment door. The uneasiness they both felt gave them cause to part early. He kissed her goodnight and promised to call tomorrow.

Planning to study for a few hours before turning in, Carla walked to the large picture window to survey the parking lot and street below. She convinced herself that it was just an unusually quiet Monday night. It was the only sense she could make of it.

Rising early the following morning after an uneasy sleep, Carla made a pot of coffee and poured herself a cup. Coffee in hand, she walked the few steps to the end table and turned on the radio. A resounding baritone voice reported:

"Orangeburg has had its first race riot. There has been quite a bit of damage near the college campus and at the bowling lanes. More than 500 students were involved. It started because Negroes were refused entrance to the bowling lanes."[4]

Stunned and feeling helpless, she ached in an empty sadness. She gazed aimlessly about the four walls that held the confinement of her concerns. She could only hope that no one was seriously hurt.

Carla's two conflicting worlds had collided. All she really wanted was four peaceful months—just four out of twelve. In her heart she knew she couldn't escape. She understood now peace at the price of another's freedom was a peace not worth having. No tradeoff was acceptable.

Streets in many cities across the nation were erupting in violence. Orangeburg was now one of them. It had joined the racial restlessness that surged across this nation.

Staying in the apartment the entire day, she tried to study and prepare for her evening class. Between calls from Stan, Mary T, and other concerned friends inquiring about her safety, it had become

---

[4]C.R. Mancari, Taped Radio Announcement, Orangeburg SC, 6 February 1968.

difficult to concentrate on her studies. At 3:00 P.M., the phone rang for the umpteenth time.

"Yes?" An impatient Carla answered.

"Hello, Carla," a distressed voice identified himself. "This is the dean. Have you heard anything about the disturbance at the bowling alley last night?"

"Yes, dean," a more quiet, reserved Carla responded, "I heard about it this morning over the radio."

"Are you coming to campus to attend your class tonight?" A tinge of fear was in his voice.

"Yes, I am," a determined Carla informed the dean.

The dean's troubled voice pleaded, "Carla, please don't come on campus."

His genuine caring for her safety touched her, but Carla wasn't about to give in to fear. The students were her friends, and she wasn't doing anything that would deny that reality.

"Dean, I want to attend my class. I think it's important that I do," Carla insisted. "I'll be all right."

The dean knew Carla well enough to know when she had decided to do something she would do it.

"All right, Carla," he sighed, "but please, wear dark makeup," he suggested.

"And Carla," he reminded her," do you remember what I told you to say if anyone should lay a hand on you?"

"Yes, sir, I do. I'll say, 'I'm soul too.'"

"Right. Be careful out there, Carla."

He was caring and kind. Carla's heart was full. At a time when so many critical problems were facing him, he took the time to call to remind her that if trouble threatened she was to say "I'm soul, too." When the dean first shared that with her last semester, she hadn't heard the term before. Now, she was hearing the term used on campus among black students.

"Soul too," she reasoned, wasn't entirely wrong for her to use. She was a member of a fine community of students whom she cared for and who cared for her. If who and what she was could be found in the heart, and not the percentage of black heritage, she indeed was "soul too."

Arriving on campus for her Tuesday evening class, Carla parked the car, and walked the few blocks through the darkness to the three story classroom building. Danger lurked.

Just a few blocks away from the campus, a large group of State and Claflin College students for the second night in a row were confronting the operator at the bowling alley. Police swung clubs, rocks flew and the plate glass windows of an automobile showroom shattered while Carla walked.

Nine people, including a policeman, were taken to the regional hospital. Ten to twelve people were arrested. The crowd was dispersed. It was happening while Carla walked.

Her heart beat fast. She hurried her pace to the safety of the lightly populated building. Quickly she climbed the two flights of stairs and entered an already-filled classroom.

Professor Polite rose from his desk, walked to the center front of the room and, in his usual soft, steady voice said, "I'm glad you're all here tonight." The full attention of every student in the room zeroed in on him. Raising and lowering his right hand as if to give weight to what he was about to say, he looked intently at the anxious students. He knew why they were here and what it was they wanted to hear from him. He complied, "Tonight, we're going to dispense with our usual class and talk about the events of yesterday evening. I'm sure some of you, if not all, have questions to ask."

Instantly, the room was filled with chatter and the question to which everyone wanted an answer: What happened? What really happened last night?

Maintaining his composure and without raising his voice, he said, with elbows bent and palms slightly facing the class in a pushing motion, "All right now, all right. Let's settle down. We'll discuss this whole incident. I'll share what I know."

The students were relieved that he would discuss the incident with them. The chatter quieted and order in the classroom was restored. Professor Polite spoke uninterrupted.

"To avoid integrating the bowling alley, just five blocks from the college campus, the operator calls it a private club. Last night, one of the white male students from State College, who isn't a member of his private club, obtained lanes without showing or being asked to show a membership card. Black students from State College followed closely behind him. They requested lanes for their use. They were denied on the pretense that 'this is a private club.'"

The hushed silence and rapt attention of the students told the professor they were eager to know what followed. How did the riot happen?

Professor Polite continued, "After the students were denied, picket lines were formed outside. Things soon got out of hand. Rocks were thrown. Windows were broken at the bowling alley and at several nearby businesses. Property was destroyed. The police estimate 500 students were involved. At the present time, this is all I know."

"Do they know if they were all from State College?" Brenda asked.

"At this time we can't be sure. Many of the students may have been from Claflin College," he answered.

William probed, "Professor, do they know the students who did the damage?"

"No, William. Cleveland Sellers may have taken part in it. Many students tried to avoid further trouble. There really is no more that I can tell you." Stirring restlessness enveloped the class.

"Professor, what is the white man afraid of anyway? What does he think we'll take away from him?" An angry Louis wanted to know.

"A nigger will marry his daughter," shouted a contemptuous Allen.

"No. No," Professor Polite insisted. Then, with a semblance of a smile, he corrected, "It's not his daughter that concerns him. It's his wife's daughter."

Laughter filled the room, breaking the overbearing tension. Carla was puzzled. She didn't have the vaguest idea what the professor was talking about. It sounded like an inside joke to which she wasn't privy.

Professor Polite noticed the dumbfounded look on her face and gently explained his comments. "You see, Carla, the white man doesn't mind a nigger marrying his daughter by his black woman, but he fears and strongly opposes even the thought of a nigger marrying his daughter by his white wife.

"A white man doesn't care what happens to his daughter by a black woman but will kill at the idea of a nigger ever marrying his daughter by his white wife. In his white mind, one has human worth, the other doesn't."

Carla's discomfort with that idea was obvious. Brenda, who sat to her left, leaned toward her and quietly whispered the name of a white Senator and said, "He has a daughter who graduated from State College. Yes, a Negro. And he paid all of her expenses while she was here." Brenda tried to assure Carla that this was true among the least expected.

This white Senator who was a dedicated segregationist and an admired public figure in the state of South Carolina, had a Negro daughter? It was difficult to believe. Carla had always believed him to be a staunch segregationist. Amazing! She had a difficult time realizing how some men could separate their public greatness from their personal deeds. Did everyone live by two different sets of morals? She questioned her own sense of moral behavior. Was she different from these men?

Suddenly, angrily, her emotions stirred to the tragedy of sexual abuse that the black women had endured, an abuse of mind and body. And the black men—the abuse and helplessness they must have endured.

Carla was especially taken with the fact that the students could still laugh through such indignities. Looking around, she became more aware of their inner strength, their soul power—and she wasn't the least bit afraid.

Satisfied that Carla understood, Professor Polite tenderly reminded each of them, "Unless we come to understand one another, there will never be a total acceptance of our human worth. What you want from others, you must give to each other."

Class was dismissed. Carla concurred with Professor Polite, yes, they must give to each other and they have much to give.

Carla's thoughts were interrupted by a hand gently touching her arm. James looked as somber and grim as she had never seen him.

"Carla, these are difficult times for everyone."

"Yes, James, I know."

James attempted a smile and walked off. He was apologizing in his own way for what was going on. James' high-spirited nature was finding it difficult to deal with the deadly serious circumstances of the moment. She barely had slid out of her seat to rise and leave when Norton walked up with a sincere warning.

"Carla, don't take any chances. It could get worse before it gets better."

Fear renewed itself. She didn't want to believe it. "But Norton, surely, violence isn't the answer. All parties will come together and work it out."

He shook his head. He was pessimistic. "Once these things start, they take on a life of their own. The violence could be an excuse for whites to act on their latent hatred rather than focus on the cause of the riot. Just be very careful."

On the drive back to her apartment, Carla drove by the bowling alley. Through the large double glass front doors, she could see a line of law-enforcement officers in white helmets, armed with riot sticks and pistols. A scary scene. Oblivious to the second night of violent interaction just two hours prior, Carla drove on.

The following afternoon, Stan visited Carla at her apartment and he pleaded, "Carla, don't go on the campus. I'm afraid you'll get hurt."

"It's all right, I'm in no danger," she assured him.

Stan became sullen and dropped into the overstuffed chair. The corners of his full mouth turned down. He reached for Carla's hand and told her what really disturbed him.

"Carla, my daughters want nothing more to do with you."

Carla hadn't seen his two oldest girls since the luncheon at the cafeteria. She realized the girls were not wholly receptive, but she couldn't fathom what she could have possibly done to cause this reaction.

"Why? What's the problem?"

"I told them that you're attending State College. They blew a fuse when they heard you were going to a 'nigger' school. I expected opposition, but nothing like this."

While Carla desperately collected her thoughts, Stan released her hand and depressingly confessed, "I believe they were coming around to liking you fine until they heard about the school."

Apparently, Carla's attending a black school made her someone other than who she was. She was now subjected to all of the hatred and prejudice that they felt toward the black race. It was much to accept. She didn't just walk in their shoes, she lived in their skin.

The weight of both her worlds overwhelmed her. Carla dropped down hard on the couch, Stan rose from his chair, sat beside her, wrapped his arms around her and held her close for a long time. They were lost in their closeness, hoping they could make it all go away.

Carla found her voice. "Your daughters are young and still missing their mother. In time, things will work out." She wasn't sure if she was speaking to Stan or herself.

Her two conflicting worlds were in a thousand pieces. Could she pick up the pieces and make them fit into one compromising world of tolerance and understanding? There was no way for her to be sure.

Stan reminded Carla they were meeting with his married friends the following evening for dinner. They embraced and he left. Carla had no time to wallow in despair. She had to quickly prepare herself for a meeting being held on campus by the student body president.

He called the meeting to order and discussed a boycott of the downtown businesses, a march to Columbia and how the students were being treated at the school infirmary. He gave the students an update on what was happening off and on campus.

"Last night we had another night of violence in front of the bowling alley. We're furious over reports that police officers beat coeds last night at the shopping center."

The second night of violence came as a surprise to Carla. She was so steeped in her "other world" of conflict that she hadn't listened to the radio this morning in fear of more turmoil.

The student body president proceeded with the update. "Violence continues in Orangeburg and in the surrounding streets. We had a disruption within a block of the school. Students from here and Claflin roamed the streets throwing rocks. Several cars were overturned. A policeman was injured when he was struck on the head with a length of pipe. Two students were treated at the hospital for injuries."

The report caused an instant outburst reaction from the students. The student president called for order. He then continued with the results of the violence from last night's riot. "Students threw rocks and bricks at passing cars. Several cars were struck. The National Guard was ordered out to protect the shopping center."

Incredible! Carla thought. All this was happening while she was going to class last night. But there's more, much more.

"Three Claflin College students were taken to the emergency room with gunshot wounds."

That caused another outburst from the audience. They wanted to know, "What's being done about the student abuse and the civil rights violations?"

"The local council and the governor's office are meeting. They can't seem to come up with an agreement whether the bowling alley is covered under the 1964 Civil Rights Act.

"The snack bar is the point of contention. If it's considered a restaurant, the lanes must be open to all. But the bowling alley operator is determined to remain a 'white only' establishment. We've been trying for some time now to work this out peacefully. We're continuing to meet with the local officials to work this out and to get a more definitive legal answer."

The meeting ended with the certainty of a student march to the state capitol in Columbia. Carla hurried to meet James at the library. He was haggard, visibly shaken. "James, is it true? Did the police beat several students?" Carla needed to hear it from another source.

"Yes, they did. They hurt them bad. Smitty said he never saw anything like it. A policeman held a female student while another policeman beat her. Carla, he said it was a battlefield. They had billy clubs a block long and used them with brutal force. After class last night, I visited with the students who were at the hospital. It made me sick."

"James, is Smitty all right?" Carla was concerned for the tall young student who often displayed his tender side whenever female students were around. He was a respectful young man and was well-liked by both male and female students.

"Yeah, he's OK, but he's upset. Man, it's not supposed to be this way. The brothers and sisters went there in peace to bowl. It's our rights we're talking about. What are we supposed to do, turn our backs and say, 'It all right massa, sir' and shuffle off to a corner and hide? No more, Carla, no more."

Carla had never seen this tough, determined side of James. They were sitting on the large cushioned chairs across from each other. James took a couple of deep breaths and continued.

"I heard the college president was all over the place last night, but he couldn't get through to those hard-nosed bigots who call themselves law and order. They're 'raw and disorder.'"

Carla momentarily closed her eyes and felt a sinking feeling within her. Her dark eyes returned their focus on an agitated James. "What do you plan to do now, James?"

"A meeting is being held in ten minutes at a professor's house. Smitty and I are going to see if they can come up with a plan to protect our brothers and sisters. The bowling alley is closed tonight. You watch yourself, Carla. It's crazy out there."

James quickly got up and left the library. Carla worried for James and his friend Smitty, both caring, sensitive individuals. Carla's mind stalled in disbelief. In the space of three days, the fires of hell had been lit. The flames were spreading and everyone may be burned.

Thursday morning, 8 February 1968. The president of South Carolina State College sent a memo warning the student body their personal safety was in jeopardy. He appealed to the students who were on the periphery of the college grounds, throwing bricks and bottles at passing traffic, to remain on campus and refrain from the negative behavior.

The same morning, Carla and her classmates were present in Professor Sammy's class. The effects of several days of stressful events showed on the faces of the students.

An unusually subdued Professor Sammy stood before the students and warned, "The violence is increasing in intensity. Cars are being overturned. Fires flare up mysteriously. Firemen are shot at while trying to put out fires. A group of militants rocked and turned over a black professor's car when he stopped at an intersection."

"Was he seriously hurt?" several students asked.

"No one knows yet. But let me warn you, things are completely out of hand. The rioters don't care about color. They attack anything and anyone who comes into their path. Sporadic sniper firing has been reported at both State College and Claflin College. Please be very careful. The situation is out of control. Our lives are being radically altered."

It disturbed Carla that the campus was in danger. She didn't want to see anyone hurt. She didn't want their lives disrupted. It was too late for that wish.

Class was dismissed. As Carla walked the few blocks to her car, she noticed angry, frustrated students milling about. Strange cars were nosing around on campus, probably reporters.

As Carla drove off the campus, she saw a crowd of whites gathering and walking toward the school entrance. Their automobiles were parked perpendicular to the front of the campus' grassy-slopes. Police cars lined up and National Guardsmen were patrolling.

It took on the appearance of a late-night parade, but it was a far more deadly event. Whether intentional or not, the spectators were sending the message to the rioters, "Come on out. You have an audience." It created an inharmonious symphony of diabolical confusion and turmoil that could only end in a discordant violence.

Making a left turn, she accelerated to the safety of her apartment, while the sirens from approaching police cars filled the air.

It had been a day filled with stress and uncertainty. Now she had to prepare for Stan's arrival. After the dreadful news Stan had given her yesterday, Carla wasn't sure she would ever see him again.

Her attention was divided between two distinct fears—the fear of more racial violence and the fear of losing Stan. The effects the demonstrations and riots were having on their relationship filled her heart with utter terror.

It was a relief when she heard Stan's soft tapping on the door. Stan appeared much more self-assured. His good looks conveyed an air of confidence. He was the Stan with whom Carla was hopelessly in love, the one who was crucial to her happiness.

They shared a long embrace. Stan kissed Carla hard on the mouth, pressing her close. Carla breathlessly whispered, "Oh, Stan I'm so glad to see you, to feel you. I wasn't sure after what you told me yesterday that I would see you again. How's your family? Is the situation any better?"

Releasing her, he held her hands in his. "Carla, my family wants me to give you up." Carla winced. He assured her, "What they want doesn't make any difference in the way I feel about you. I love you too much to let them interfere with our plans. I can handle it." Stan seemed so sure, so resolute. How could she doubt him? Why should she worry? But she did.

The ride to the restaurant was pleasant. Stan looked forward to her meeting his friends at dinner. Stan's friends were aware that Carla attended State College and she knew that they shared the racial attitudes of many of the whites in Orangeburg.

Placed in an awkward position, Stan's friends were visibly uncomfortable, but for Stan's sake they did the best they could to cope. Their conversation tactfully avoided the absurdity of the situation. The entire evening centered on stock car racing and the couple's six-month-old son. It was a long, boring evening.

As they pretended all was well in their narrow white world, a group of students, one of them Smitty, set a bonfire in front of the grassy slopes at State College. Firemen rushed to extinguish the blaze, National Guardsmen occupied the street near the college and police squads formed a firing line at the entrance. The players were in place. The stage was set.

Dinner over, they said goodnight to Stan's friends. Driving back toward Carla's apartment, Stan believed the evening went well. Pleased with his friends' acceptance of Carla, he smiled, and was relaxed.

Carla was just glad the evening was over. All she really wanted was to spend quiet time with Stan—to be alone with him, to snuggle into the curves of his strong arms.

Within a block of the apartment, they were taken by surprise by a barricade guarded by several National Guardsmen.

"Evening, folks," one politely greeted them. "We've had a problem. You can't drive through this area."

Stan was irate. He insisted, "We need to drive through."

The Guardsman was firm. "The entire area here is closed, sir. No one may enter."

"What do you mean, I can't drive through? I've a right to go wherever I want!" Stan was visibly angry. He gripped the steering wheel tightly with both hands, his shoulders stiffened and jaw muscles quivered. "This woman lives in that apartment building right ahead of us."

The Guardsman calmly repeated, "This entire area is closed, sir. No one may enter."

Raising his voice, a frustrated Stan didn't give up. "Just how the sam-hell do you expect her to get to her apartment?"

Another guardsman, hearing the commotion, joined the exchange of words. They discussed it between themselves, and finally agreed to allow Stan to drive through—at his own risk.

Stan parked in front of Carla's apartment building. Frightened by the ordeal, Carla commented, "Stan, something serious must be going on." "Nah," Stan casually remarked, "probably just the darned colored people acting up again. Have to keep them in their place."

Astounded, Carla couldn't understand how Stan could only moments before become angry because he thought his rights were being infringed upon—the same rights that he would deny blacks. He was upset because the students wanted what was rightfully theirs. Stan actually believed he had certain rights, but they did not. He believed it.

However, as concerned as she was, her love and yearning for this man were greater. They were so totally involved with each other that it was as though no one else existed. What they were doing was creating a third world for themselves to love in. They were so busy protecting their relationship, neither one of them wanted to look left nor right, in fear of seeing the reality of events surrounding them.

The evening events were disconcerting. They had agreed to end the evening as soon as Carla was safely at home. Carla walked to the large picture window and watched as Stan drove his way back through the barricade. A sorrowful moan escaped her lips. "Oh, Stan, how can I deny what is the best part of me—the love of people, all people, and it's the blacks who have taught me this. How can I possibly ever again deny them their humanity? Whatever is true of them is true of me. To put any human being down would be to put myself down. To degrade one is to degrade all. Oh, my love, how are you to understand this?"

For the moment at least, the parking lot below presented the appearance of a calm peace. Nothing moved.

But the night didn't remain silent. Sirens continued to pierce the apartment walls as they had for the last three nights—the god-awful sirens, *shrilling, screeching, piercing*—the sound of unfolding catastrophe grew ever-louder and ever more insistent.

15

Blood On the Grassy Slopes

Haunted by sirens, Carla awoke at 6:00 AM from a restless sleep. Rolling over onto her back, she stretched her arm full-length over her head to the end table and turned on the radio. She anxiously grasped and turned the knob.

"Three Students have been killed; Two guardsmen wounded. And many others were wounded during last night's riot at the entrance of State College. At this time, no one knows exactly what happened. We will come back to this story just as soon as we have further information."[5]

Carla's worst fears were realized. She lay on the bed in complete disbelief. The terse announcement sent a shock wave through her entire body. As she struggled feebly to move, there was a slow-motion feel to it. She sat up on the edge of the bed and attempted to comprehend what it was that she had just heard. Three students dead? Rebelling at the horror, it was difficult to reconcile her scattered thoughts. Heaven's light dimmed, tender choices lost in a maze of hatred.

In a state of shock, she denied what had happened. However, there were parents out there who couldn't deny the gravity of their heartfelt loss. The light of their lives extinguished forever.

Not having a television, Carla spent the morning glued to the radio. The news announcer repeated the reports of the deaths again

---

[5]C.R. Mancari, Taped Radio Announcement, Orangeburg SC, 9 February 1968.

and again, but details were scarce. Fortunately, she had no classes today or this evening. At home, she tried to re-engage her thought processes. The constant phone calls of concern for her welfare served to reinforce the reality of the radio reports.

In the afternoon, Carla purposely drove around Orangeburg. She talked with some of the local businessmen. Understandably, they were scared, most believed the actions of the students were all "so unnecessary."

Carla wondered if the rights and privileges were denied these business people, would they have still considered it as all "so unnecessary?" Obviously, they believed civil rights had color—a white color. The white community was told they must close their stores early, and they weren't to go out at night. They considered it an infringement of their basic civil white rights, and they believed no one should be able to infringe upon them.

What Carla wanted to say was, put the shoe on the other foot, put yourselves in their place. Basic civil rights—isn't that what the rioters were asking for? How do they get what was rightfully theirs when they had begged and pleaded and were abused and ignored? Then, when they couldn't take it anymore, they exploded in pent-up rage. We were judging and degrading them, because violence was unacceptable. It was what she wanted to say. However, Carla exited the premises quietly.

She knew violence of any kind wasn't the answer, but in the students' place, how would they get what was rightfully theirs? Maybe the whites, too, would come out fighting. They almost have to admire people who were willing to die for what they believed in, willing to die for the rights and privileges that whites took for granted. Yes, as angry as the whites were, they had to admire the students. Carla did.

Picking up the local newspaper, the *Times and Democrat*, Friday, 9 February 1968, in large bold print the headline read:

"ALL HELL BREAKS LOOSE—THREE KILLED, MANY WOUNDED IN COLLEGE NIGHTMARE." It followed with additional details.

A steady stream of automobiles left the college campus bearing the dying and wounded to the hospital and, as each started to leave the college grounds, the lawmen and newspaper reporters were warned to take cover. Snipers had been shooting from cars leaving the campus "And, in the belief that perhaps all of the casualties had not been found, police cars later traveled the roads and even the lawn of the college, their headlights and spotlights peering into places where dead or wounded may have fallen.

The national association for the advancement of colored people requested from the justice department national guardsmen from neutral areas outside of south carolina to guarantee safety of negro citizens and students.

Included was a picture of a television crew on the ground watching the scene of violence. Another, a firing line of State Patrolmen, cutting loose a volley of fire at the rioters on the grassy slopes. And, the most telling of all, a large picture of three State Patrolmen as they looked down on two of the dead students who laid—mortally wounded where they had fallen. Their shoes were in disarray next to their lifeless bodies.

The paper scrunched in Carla's hands, she darted back to her apartment. Dropping the newspaper on the end table, she threw herself on the sofa. In wonderment, she asked herself, how could it have come to this?

Even by 8:00 PM, the radio news accounts still reported very little accurate information about the previous night's riot. One fact remained; three teenaged black male youths were dead. One was a seventeen-year-old high school student who had a brother at State College. Many others were injured. Rumors ran rampant while fear multiplied. No one knew exactly what had happened. Even those who witnessed it told different stories. Everyone wanted to know, "Who shot first?"

The police and National Guard insisted that they were fired upon first. The students were adamant that no shots were fired except by the police and National Guard.

The only thing that seemed definite was that a police officer was hit across the face by a student with a board. As the policeman fell, the police and Guardsmen thought he had been shot, and someone yelled, "Fire!" As shots rang out, three teenage students had fallen to the earth, leaving the cause for which they died seared into the minds and souls of their fellow students.

The nine o'clock news brought word that the entire community was closed down and under curfew.

Whirring and clanging sounds of sirens and fire trucks raced past the apartment building all evening. The telephone rang constantly. Stan and many of Carla's other friends again expressed concern for her safety. Mary T wanted her to return to Charleston. With class term papers to finish, Carla felt she needed to stay, despite the closed college.

A distraught Stan defied curfew to visit with Carla. He cautioned, "Please, Carla, don't go near the campus. The National Guard has the situation under control." He said nothing about the race riots or the appalling tragedy.

Stan's mental energies were consumed by what it was he believed he wanted for himself. He made a commitment. "Carla, I want you to attend a family dinner next week at my mother's house."

"I've told my mother that I intend to marry you. She knows that once my mind is made up, there's no stopping me, so she wants to get to know you." Stan sat on the sofa, pulled Carla down to sit beside him.

Carla's mind and heart were spinning out of control. In just five days, events had redefined her life forever. Her two conflicting worlds had collided and now a new world was forged before her eyes. Could this be really happening now? Now, when her heart was being tugged at in a place she never knew existed.

They embraced. He leaned back on the sofa, and held her close.

The room was very warm. Although charged with desire, the desperate wailing of the fire trucks and police sirens brought them back to the reality of Orangeburg. They stopped. Stan sat up, smiled, took her hands to his lips and kissed her fingers. They sat quietly, their rhythmic breathing subsided and their rational minds regained control of their bodies.

Carla's concern for their future weighed heavily on her heart. Their racial views would always lurk in the shadows of their passion. Stan's strength was in his all-consuming belief in himself. Carla had to also rely on that belief. Her strength was long overtaxed.

Stan was quick to reassure her, "Don't worry, Carla, we'll get through this. We love each other enough to work it out. No one, including my family, will ever interfere with what we have."

Carla wanted to believe what they had together was stronger than what either one of them could possibly have separately. Together they could withstand family doubts—but only together.

Stan lightly touched Carla's cheek, intently looked into the spirit of her trusting dark eyes. "I'm not giving you up. My family realizes that now. Be patient with them. They'll come around. You'll see."

They hugged and Stan got up to leave. Stan was in the middle, too, caught between his family, his racial loyalty and his love for Carla. He was handling a demanding situation the best he knew how. The room was cold and empty without him.

Carla glanced at her watch, 11:00 P.M. Both wanting to know the latest news and dreading it, she turned on the radio.

To Carla, the radio reports sounded like the politicians were looking for someone to blame. She recorded, "What is getting lost in the translation is the contemptible manner in which the blacks are treated. This didn't just "happen." It has been happening in a whisper for more than a hundred years. The Negro voice is loud and clear. Whites might not like the sound, but the black voice would never be mute again."

Carla remembered she once tried to fix blame on the Black Awareness Organization. She knew how much easier it was, and a lot less painful, to point a finger in another direction.

Carla, too, fought the battle of blame, and whether she won or lost the battle, it brought the agonizing pain of change. These tragic events brought to the surface the full reality of change. This same change confronted an entire nation.

Left with the feeling of numbed sadness, Carla breathed a heavy sigh and thought aloud, "Why, oh God? Why did it ever have to come this far? Why couldn't we, I, read the signs, heard the sounds before these precious beings, mothers' sons, were shot down because they had the courage to have their voices heard. They had the courage to say justice now.

"No one in this nation should ever have to commit an act of violence to claim what is rightfully his. The three young men would never have been standing in a position to kill or be killed if racial hatred wasn't still a fact of racial reality in this city and in this nation. The three young men paid a dear price." Carla hoped that it paid for the civil rights of those who were being denied.

Having been a victim herself, Carla understood the diseased mind that hatred and fear created. She recorded, "Hatred, fear and violence were insidious. They breed from each other, urge each other on and change men, women, and children into beasts. Hatred stored up between the races who have lived together in more or less peaceful manner for so many years causes fear.

"No real peace exists. No harmony. Beneath the stillness lurks the demon fear that spreads violence like a plague upon the land.

"There is a sword with which to slay the demon. Its name: justice. But justice is another name for equality, and equality is a frightening thing to those who believe that giving others their God-given due means taking something essential from themselves."

Saturated with news of more force, maintenance, and containment, Carla turned the radio off and prepared for a much-needed rest.

She awakened at dawn's first light. With an inner tug at her heart, she was drawn to the school campus. The school was officially closed, but a part of her still wanted to believe that the catastrophic collision of her two worlds had never happened.

Carla drove the short distance to the campus entrance, turned right and drove past the grassy slopes, now bloodstained, the same grassy slopes that welcomed her onto the campus so many times. Now the grassy slopes remained an epitaph to an irreplaceable loss.

She parked the car, and slowly walked to the building where her Saturday morning class was usually held. She thought how eerie and quiet Orangeburg had been the night Stan and she drove back from Columbia. But it didn't compare to the stillness this morning. Entering the open space beneath the three story classroom, she contemplatively climbed the familiar two flights of stairs to the third level. Walking to the center of the concrete landing, with its iron railing running its full length, she grasped the rail with both hands. The iron rail, like the weather, was cold. Leaning forward, she viewed her beloved campus.

The only sound was the wind. On the ground below a small piece of white paper stirred about as a gentle breeze played with it. No one was around. No young people talking or laughing. It was as though the whole world had died.

She could see across the large parking lot to the main street. Drifting her sight to the right, she surveyed the cafeteria, the administration building, the Annie Williams' dormitory, the mechanical building, the post office, the men's dorms. She searched for signs of life—not another car or person could be seen.

So loud was the silence that she wanted to cover her ears. So isolated was this black world that she wanted to cover her face with her hands and shut her eyes. Her coming here a year ago was a selfish decision. Her coming here this morning was a journey of the heart.

Something had ended. Something had died. Carla hoped that beyond the three young students who had died here, the hatred and prejudice that existed in this city and nation died with them.

All was dismal, her eyes watered and tears flowed. Last summer, she had cried for herself, but this morning she cried for all—black and white.

In the solitude of her apartment, Carla desperately sought a release from the volatile events. However, in the corners of her mind, there was no place to hide. The overburden emotional force contorted and replayed the horror of the moments. Carla wished she could return to her childhood inner world of silence, but it was in a distant past and the pathway had long since become obscured. She had ventured too far into the reality of time and space.

Driving downtown to a restaurant where she sometimes had breakfast, she parked the car and walked the few steps to the door. Her attention was drawn to the news stand in front of its entrance. Purchasing the *Times and Democrat,* Carla glanced at the predictable screaming headlines.

Entering the restaurant, she sat alone at the counter and ordered a cup of coffee. Her shoulders sagged as she scanned the disturbing front page large bold headlines.

NATIONAL GUARDSMEN AND HEAVY ARMOR ON
GUARD NEAR ENTRANCE TO COLLEGES

ORANGEBURG IS A CITY OF SILENCE

CAMPUSES VIRTUALLY DESERTED[6]

It was pretty much what she had been bombarded with for the last two days. As her interest in the written page lessen, she was distracted by scraps of conversations around her. Among the white patrons there was a rousing resentment. Sinking inside, her heart began to pound.

"It's outside agitators," one man insisted.

"They're the perpetrators," another agreed.

"Terrible business, really terrible. But what could the police do?"

"If the outsiders would go away, everything would be all right."

They were in the grips of hatred where reason and fairness were overshadowed. It was alarmingly difficult to absorb. She wanted so desperately to hear some recognition of the behavior of the white community toward the students. None was heard.

A flashback to a year ago reminded Carla she had been exactly as the people sitting around her this morning. She couldn't condemn them, her concern was also for them. They were struggling to hold

---

[6]The *Times and Democrat,* Orangeburg SC, 10 February 1968.

on to past attitudes. Carla understood they spoke from an accumulation of myths and false beliefs that evoked hostile verbal attacks. She knew they would be different if they had her exposure, her gift of having black friends.

If the white people of Orangeburg and the nation attended State College with her, sat beside her classmates, listened to them and talked with them, they couldn't possibly dislike them.

But they didn't know them. Carla did. There she sat, surrounded by her white world, looking out from within her "black world." She felt inadequate because she couldn't reach the people on the outside any more than she could've been reached by blacks a year ago. She scolded herself for being totally irrational. The solution to the racial problem disturbed her more than anything else.

Taking a sip of the hot coffee, replacing the cup onto its hair-cracked saucer, her heart fluttered. As once before, a long time ago, she couldn't stay to finish a cup of coffee. Tossing a dollar on the counter, she left in haste.

Driving from the restaurant toward her apartment, she questioned how racial issues could be resolved? What was the solution? People couldn't be forced to like each other, get to know one another. They cannot be dragged along kicking and screaming. The solution was a critical one, because Carla was aware that it was the same solution that must be found for her and Stan.

Tuesday, 13 February, the front page of the *Times and Democrat* covered the funeral held in Orangeburg for the seventeen year-old high school student who was slain Thursday evening.

A picture showed his grieving brother, a State College student so distraught with grief he could hardly walk. As he was helped by friends, tears streamed down his face.

The communication gap widened between the students and the white community as they each made their demands.

Students at "white" Furman College carried placards and marched in front of the federal building in Greenville, South Carolina, protesting the killings of the three students at South

Carolina State College. They stood up for and supported the three fallen students.

On Wednesday, Carla worked for a few hours at the employment office. Her co-workers were more distant. They bordered on rudeness. Sandra could no longer afford to associate with Carla. Peer pressure dictated her relationships. White or black, peer pressure was peer pressure. Carla understood and didn't pursue it.

Finally, at the end of the second week, the National Guard was withdrawn from the entrance of the college. The biracial committee continued to work on the students' grievances. With the passage of time, it was becoming a futile exercise. The students weren't seeing any immediate changes.

Sunday morning Carla dressed, walked down the street a few blocks to a newsstand to pick up the paper. The headline read:

SITUATION STILL DANGEROUS; JUSTICE DEPARTMENT WILL SUE—AND, THEY ALL WANT TO KNOW WHO FIRED FIRST SHOT[7]

Back at the apartment, Carla poured herself a cup of coffee, and quietly reviewed the latest reporting.

The state of emergency extended to all of Orangeburg county. A large picture of a Washington newsman injured while on the State College grounds dominated the page.

Local businesses complained they were suffering economically from the curfew. More than 700 students met to discuss a boycott of all white businesses. Carla thought that would surely add to the business community's problems. County and city leaders claimed they weren't aware of the Black Power Awareness on the campuses. Their energies remained fixed on finding fault with the students.

The governor's concern rested on the national tarnished image of South Carolina. "The years of work and understanding have been shattered by this unfortunate incident at Orangeburg. Our

---

[7]Ibid., 11 February 1968.

reputation for racial harmony has been blemished by the actions of those who would place selfish motives and interests above the welfare and security of the majority."[8] What understanding?

Weary of the news stories, Carla turned in early with the hope that somehow the dark room would soothe her heartache and rest her mind. It didn't help.

The next day Stan took time off of work to have lunch with Carla. He wanted her to know, "The family dinner at my mother's house is postponed until curfew ends. I'm confident the white establishment can handle and control the racial unrest." Stan didn't want to believe change was inevitable. His world must remain "white only."

The following morning, Carla returned to the same restaurant she had visited two weeks earlier. She sat alone at the counter and again ordered a cup of coffee. The people sitting around were all puffed up with themselves. They were open and direct with their views on the past weeks' events.

A group of six sitting at a table near her shouted across to another table, "I'll tell you or anyone else that Orangeburg can handle these niggers! We showed them by the killings what they'll get if they fool around with us." The entire restaurant broke out in laughter. Others began to join in.

The consensus was pretty much in agreement with what had just been said. Carla didn't see or hear the least bit of change in their racial attitudes. These local people wanted to quiet the students and have them crawl back into their submissive, dark corners. They were happy as long as the students were barely seen and hardly heard. Let everything go on as it was before the riots, unequal and separate. Let's go back to "business as usual."

With all of the talking and good intentions of the peacemakers, no one seemed to be listening. Talk about a lack of communication. The lines of communication weren't just down, they were never up!

---

[8]Ibid., 81.

What shocked and disturbed Carla the most was that last summer, she would've thought the same. Carla left another cup of coffee behind.

Fifteen days after the riots, Claflin College reopened. Three days later, South Carolina State College reopened. Many of the 1,500 students returned. The bowling lanes remained closed.

The curfew was lifted. The tense atmosphere on campus gradually subsided. Students appeared cautiously relaxed. Carla was glad to be back to the task for which she was here, and to see her classmates.

A week later, a meeting was held in the school auditorium. That same evening, Carla attended Professor Polite's class and he informed the students about the results of the meeting.

"A plan is in the works for several busloads of South Carolina State College students to demonstrate at the state capitol. I'm not only afraid, I'm downright scared. The meeting that was held earlier today was very rough. The young people became extremely militant. In fact, they could've put Carmichael and H. Rap Brown to shame. They plan to take over the local organization. The killings have made them even more radical—if that is possible."

The other white student in the class asked, "Professor, is it safe for a white student to come on and off the campus?" The students burst into laughter.

Carla's inner plea was, please don't make this so personal. She hadn't been afraid, but this white student's fear could become hers.

Professor Polite quieted the laughter and reminded the students, "The young people are threatening to take three white lives. I also have had a basketful of threats. The youth believe that I'm an Uncle Tom who stands in their way. They want me removed from the faculty or they threaten to do it themselves for the school."

Professor Polite was almost in tears, "I don't want to get in their way. However, none of us can afford to just walk away. There will be work to do long after order has been restored. It'll take all of us getting involved to ensure permanent change and continuous progress."

His voice became steady. "It'll take white, black, non-militant and, yes, militant, to achieve a change that touches the minds and hearts of this nation. It has always been said that the young need something worth dying for, the old need something worth living for. Now both have something to die for. It requires them both in their own time to balance the scales of justice in the eyes of the God who created each of us. A God who created us to care for each other without hatred."

James asked, "But, Professor, aren't you afraid for your life?"

Without hesitation, Professor Polite replied, "No, I have something to die for. What I fear most is that our people believe integration is a permanent solution. It's a beginning, not an end."

For the first time, Carla warned herself, if she isn't afraid, certainly she should be. If they would hurt one of their own, Professor Polite, a kind and gentle man, would they hesitate to hurt anyone else?

Class was dismissed in a quiet hush. A little chatter was heard among the students. They all had sensed the importance of the Professor's talk. The emptiness of helplessness overshadowed Carla's usual audaciousness.

The night was cold. The sun had set long before. Even with the campus street lights, the darkness pervaded. Carla buttoned her heavy winter coat, tossed a long wool scarf around her neck and wrapped her arms around her textbooks holding them close to her chest. She set out for the long dark walk to her car.

As she walked along, she was keenly aware of how quiet and menacing the campus had become. She thought as she passed the buildings now casting sinister shadows, why must anyone die? Why couldn't we all, young and old, live for each other? Then, the scales of justice would always be balanced. There she was again, always trying to simplify everything. Had she forgotten that truth was full of contradictions in its explanations.

Suddenly, footsteps interrupted her thoughts. It sounded like several men coming up from behind her. Just ahead of her, in a darkened corner between two buildings, several angry male voices spoke loudly in confrontation.

Cold stark fear took over. Her heart palpitated. Her forehead throbbed, her brain froze. She didn't dare turn around. Anxious to reach her car she hurried her pace.

Within moments, two black men walked up, one on each side of her. They said not a word—not even to each other. She was totally vulnerable, a petite, five-foot three-inch, 105-pound white woman carrying an armful of books. All she could think was, keep walking, Carla, keep walking.

16

Courage is Caring

After what seemed like an eternity, she dared to make eye contact with the one on her left. She recognized him. It was James. He gave her a reassuring, protective glance. The other was a student from their class. What in the world? Instantly, Carla knew they were going out of their way, acting as her personal guardian angels, making sure she made it safely to her car.

They approached her car. Carla unlocked the door, and slid into the driver's seat. Glancing up at them, Carla wanted very much to tell them how much she appreciated their kind gesture, how much she cared for them. But no words came forth. The tears in her eyes and the lump in her throat were larger than any words she could possibly say.

They understood and appreciatively smiled. Quickly, they went back the way they had come, without a word ever being spoken.

Driving off campus, part of Carla wondered if she really had anything to fear? Or was she deliberately tossing all thoughts of fear out of her mind? However, it was difficult to fear people she had come to know and care about.

Carla still found it hard to believe that any harm would come to her. She saw such caring love in the young men's eyes tonight. That was something worth dying for. She understood what Professor Polite had been trying to say. Yes, there was a cause here worth dying for. In his quiet way, his caring courage touched all of them this night. Courage was caring.

The following evening, Carla cleared her head for a visit with Stan and the baby, Cathy. The time she spent with the little one was less time for brooding. The baby's laughter and spontaneous good nature lifted Carla's spirits during the worst of times.

The visit with Cathy and Stan was enjoyable. Cathy's sweet innocence at least momentarily gave Carla the relief she sought.

With the visit and studying behind her, Carla called it a night. The past weeks had been horrendous. She looked forward to the beginning of a new week with the anticipation of both her worlds meshing in a peaceful reconciliation.

Sunday was a cold, bright sunny day. Carla awakened to a familiar phone ring. Stan wanted to say, "Good morning, sleepy head. The baby loves being with you almost as much as I do." Stan knew all of the right buttons to push.

Carla yawned, wrinkled her nose, smiled and in a sleepy voice said, "She's all beauty and sweetness, Stan. I love her giggle. She breaks me up."

"Carla, get some rest today and I'll call again later. Love you sweetheart."

"Love you, too."

Carla spent the weekend and following week, when she wasn't studying or working, with Stan and Cathy. Stan could only refer to the racial issues in generalities. He tended to ignore the students' cry for justice. These were times when Carla was troubled by a twinge of doubt. Although her love for him remained uncompromised, she couldn't help but wonder if her emotions blurred her sense of justice.

Once again, Carla kept pace with the demands of a full schedule. And now there was the family dinner she must attend to meet Stan's mother and relatives.

Carla was a nervous wreck. Nothing looked right on her. The lack of sleep and eating had played havoc with her clothes. Nothing fit her. She changed several times. Her dark-brown shoulder-length hair needed a trim. She settled for her first choice of dress, and fussed with her hair and makeup.

The knock on the door rescued her sanity. Stan was here. He tossed his overcoat across the sofa. He was strong and handsome in his navy blue suit, white shirt and silk tie. However, there was something noticeably different about him. Carla wasn't quite sure what it was. But he had a conspiratorial glint in his clear blue eyes tonight.

He kissed her and with appraising eyes and said, "Honey, you look great. You'll knock them out." Then came the shocker.

"I have a surprise for you," he said, with a rush of pride and wide grin.

"What? What?" Carla flushed with anticipation, excitedly responded.

He reached inside his jacket and retrieved a small, dark-blue velvet box. Breathless, Carla leaped for joy. Could it be? Tantalizing Carla, Stan slowly raised its small blue top and handed it to her. In a shiver of anticipation, Carla took the small velvet box. Yesss! It was. A beautiful solitaire diamond engagement ring.

"Oh Stan," she wrapped her arms around his neck.

"Holding the ring to the light, Carla watched its sparkle.

"It's so beautiful," Carla sighed. He kissed her again, and again reminded her how much he loved her.

"Should I wear it?" She asked worriedly. "Your family will all be there. They might not like it."

Stan encircled her in his arms. Never had he felt more masculine, more strong. "Carla, we love each other. I want you to marry me and share my life. The baby loves you and the older girls will come around. Trust me. I can handle it for both of us."

"Stan, are you sure?" she asked in a low, hushed voice, stepping back from his hold.

"Yes, I am. I want you to marry me next month. We can be married in secret." Stan was staying the course. He wasn't about to place his plans in jeopardy by allowing his family the opportunity to convince him to change direction.

"Stan, I have the semester to finish. Is it wise for us to rush into it without your family knowing?" A moment of apprehension and caution temporarily trampled on her jubilant mood.

Stan, with a little weakness in his voice, soberly said, "Carla, if you finish the semester and move back to Charleston, I may lose you. I don't want to take that chance."

Reassuring Stan that would never happen, Carla moved back into the circle of his affectionate hold. As she leaned her cheek against his muscular shoulder, her heart skipped a beat. She wasn't sure if it was from the pleasant feeling of safety and permanence or the creeping doubts that flared up to threaten the moment.

Stan's presence always had a way of quickly banishing those flaring doubts. Soon, Carla was swinging around the room in gleeful contentment. Stan reached out, took hold of her wrist, slowed her pace and said, "Let's see how it fits."

Carla's lips quivered as Stan slid the ring on her finger. It was a perfect fit. Her eyes filled with tears as she looked up from the sparkling diamond ring into Stan's sparkling blue eyes. This moment was theirs. Standing by the large picture window, arms entwined, gazing at the ring's brilliance on her finger, they were lost in its dazzling promise of a lasting love.

The evening with Stan's family plodded along. The family noticed the ring immediately. However, no reference to it was made. In fact, they made every effort to ignore its sparkle the entire night.

Stan's mother made an attempt to be friendly. It was an effort of polite dislike. Stan's older girls avoided Carla as much as possible. Cathy, on the other hand, hugged and kissed her. She wanted to sit on Carla's lap the entire time.

Stan's uncles, aunts and cousins made small talk and managed to avoid referring to the past weeks of alarming events. They did their best to present a face of peaceful tranquility. The discomfort with their task was obvious. Great effort was exerted to be sure there were no slip-ups. None were made.

Stan was always close by Carla's side. She was aware of his all-embracing strength. It was as though they were facing a firing squad together. The squad could take their best shot. It wouldn't hurt them. With Stan's defiant demonstration of bucking the white order, Carla was lulled into a sense of a smug fortress. She believed that their love could survive anything.

With the all-important family gathering behind her, Carla felt closer to Stan then ever before. She believed Stan was forced to make a choice and was swearing his allegiance to her.

Quickly banishing any doubts when they arose, Carla continued to ride an emotional see-saw between the highs with Stan and the lows on campus.

In Professor Polite's class, he discussed the meetings of the bi-racial committee, a group of people who were trying to bring harmony back to Orangeburg. However, Professor Polite wasn't pleased with the way the meetings were conducted.

"How do you handle young people whom you want to positively influence if the adults at the meeting are giving bad examples of themselves by interrupting the speaker and being very rude?" he asked in an agitated voice.

The classroom was plunged into a deep silence. The students were aware that their professors were caught in the middle. They were expected to teach, keep students calm and, at the same time, work with the militants to restore order on campus. No easy job.

Professor Polite concluded, "Cool heads must prevail if we're to come out of this with any positive long-term results."

He looked tired, beaten. It was obvious that Professor Polite was seeking an elusive solution to a mind and heart-wrenching problem.

The tension and distress were reflected on the students' faces. It was felt. It was as though they were all waiting for the next incident. The class was dismissed.

Walking out of class, an attractive, light-skinned graduate student approached Carla. Tall and thin with small features, Darlene wore frameless eyeglasses and her hair combed flat and close to her head. Carla was immediately drawn to this sensitive, soft-spoken person who expressed concern for her welfare.

She extended an invitation. "Carla, I live just a short distance from the college. When you have some free time, why don't you come by to visit?" Darlene taught in public school and was married to a school principal. They had two young children. Children that Carla would look forward to visiting.

Happily, Carla accepted, and Darlene wrote down her address for her. They said goodnight, and went their separate ways. Carla was grateful for the kind gesture.

Pervaded by a quiet inner peace, Carla marveled at the idea that she had no fear of blacks. She felt as though the school was part of her now and the students were a part of her.

Carla turned to her mechanical friend and recorded, "I'm sure there are many whites who will say I'm a 'nigger lover.' I think of myself as a 'people lover.'"

Differences existed, she knew that. But as she came to appreciate the differences, a racial peace within her was attainable. The willingness to give to others the very things that she wanted for herself was what Professor Polite was talking about.

A memorial service for the three slain teenagers was held on the campus steps of White Hall. The student body turned out in force to support the fallen students.

The tragedy of Thursday evening, 8 February 1968, was referred to as the "Orangeburg Massacre" or the "Orangeburg Incident."

Buried in the news of a tumultuous year: Martin Luther King Jr.'s assassination, Robert Kennedy's assassination, the continuing war in Vietnam, and President Johnson's announcement he would not seek reelection, the "Orangeburg Massacre" received little attention in the national press, and was quickly forgotten. It only momentarily grabbed the attention of the nation. Then the attention of America moved on—to more violence.

However, for the parents of the three dead young men, for those attending South Carolina State College and for the local black community, the tragedy was not forgotten.

The date was stamped indelibly within each of their hearts, as was the memory of Delano Middleton, age seventeen, Samuel Hammond Jr., age eighteen, and Henry Smith, Smitty, age eighteen.

17

That Gentle Breeze

"Hmm."

"Is something wrong?"

All he continued to say was, "Hmm" as he manipulated the soft tissue.

February, what a month—riots in the streets, killings on the campus, and an engagement to be married. What else could possibly happen this month?

Lying on a table in Charleston, Carla was having an annual physical. The doctor frowned and grunted, one of those god-awful doctor grunts that sent shivers up your spine.

"Is something wrong?" Carla asked again.

"Carla, you have a lump," the no-nonsense doctor stated.

Abruptly, she sat up and repeated his analysis. "A lump?"

"Yes. In your right breast. I want you to enter the hospital at once. It's imperative that you have a biopsy." He left no room for discussion.

Shocked, Carla went on the defensive. "Look, Doctor Lauder, I only have a little more than two months of school left. With everything else going on in my life, I don't need another crisis."

"Carla, your health is more important," he insisted in a more forceful tone. "Let's get you into a hospital. The biopsy will be done and you'll remain under anesthesia until the results are in. If the biopsy is positive, a radical will be performed."

"A mastectomy?" she shouted. With eyes about to pop out of their sockets, she questioned, "Are you saying that I won't know if one of my breasts has been removed until I wake up after the surgery for the biopsy?"

"Yes, that's exactly what I'm saying." Doctor Lauder persisted, "And the biopsy should be done now, not two months from now." Doctor Lauder was beginning to lose patience with his incredulous patient.

"I'm sorry, Dr. Lauder, but this is all coming down on me suddenly, without the least bit of warning. I have to be back for school tomorrow. Let me talk it over with Mary T and call you later today."

"But...." Doctor Lauder protested.

"Thank you for your concern, doctor." The sharpness of Carla's voice suggested the discussion was closed.

On the drive to Mary T's, Carla's mind was heavily sedated with too much of life's tragic events. She already felt she had climbed Mt. Everest several times. What was this? A mountain she had never heard of.

Walking into the house, Carla blurted out the problem. In her usual calming voice, Mary T said, "Okay, okay, sit. We'll have a cup of coffee and talk this out." She placed the cups on the table and walked to the stove to fetch the coffee pot. After pouring the coffee, she sat down and said, "All right, Carla, let's hear what your choices are."

"Mary T, if I disobey the doctor, I'll have to live with the uncertainty of it for two months. If I leave school now, it'll mean a setback for at least a full semester. My choice isn't exactly between heaven and hell here. It's more like hell and hell. I've already paid dearly for the degree that I was supposed to get 'standing on my head.'"

Mary T smiled, trying to ease the mix of fear and frustrated tension bottled up in Carla. "Carla, you may not want to hear this, but I agree with the doctor. Your health is more important than finishing school this semester. You can always go back later. Perhaps, for the fall semester. It's only a few months' difference."

"But Mary T, I've no way of knowing in what condition the surgery will leave me and I'm afraid what I started last summer can't be finished later. I'll never be able to pick up later where I'm now in relationships and human understanding. My gut feeling, Mary T, is that there's more here at stake than the condition of my health."

Mary T sighed, arms crossed on the table with head momentarily lowered, she leaned forward and raised her eyes in disappointment. She looked Carla squarely and forcefully in the eyes as she said, "You're telling me you're going back to school tomorrow."

"Yes, I guess I am. But I promise to check into a hospital as soon as the spring semester is over."

"Well, it's your decision. I don't like it, but it's your decision to make. She added in a troubled voice, "The worst part is that this breast problem will place additional stress on you."

"Yes, I've thought of that, too, but it doesn't matter. I'm in the most important phase of my life. I want to—have to—finish what I've started. There's no turning back, not even for reasons of health. But you're right, I'm leaving Charleston with a heavier heart," Carla lamented.

Mary T refilled the coffee cups. "At least I get to finish a cup here," Carla somberly jested. They both shared a laugh. It eased the pain.

It was with sadness that Carla returned to school. Disconcertingly swept up, she felt life currents buffeted her about. Only twenty-four hours, earlier, she had left with a future certain. Now, she returned with a life uncertain.

In the early morning hours, she found herself standing in front of a mirror flattening her breast with her hand, to see how she would look without it. What she saw was a frightening reflection of her.

Carla had an impending marriage to consider. How could she tell Stan? Could she marry him now? Hasn't he had enough to cope with? Haven't they both had enough to cope with? She couldn't do this to him. He must know. She decided she would tell him when he came to visit after class tomorrow.

Lying in bed, Carla prayed aloud, "God help me, I'm scared. This does frighten me. I feel totally wiped out. This is a nightmare that I could have never imagined."

After what seemed like an endless night, Carla knew she had to gather her troubled thoughts and mustn't allow time to slip beneath her feet. Forcing yesterday's startling news to the back of her mind, she attended Professor Sammy's morning class.

Professor Sammy informed them about an interesting development involving the biracial meetings. In an unusually low-keyed tone, he began, "The whites who were attending the meeting were asked to leave the room. All of the whites got up and left the room except for one man. The white man who remained in the room was one who actually lives and works in the black community.

"He was identifying himself with the blacks. In his mind, he would never have believed that he would be asked to leave the room. However, several of the blacks became very upset and angry with him, and told him that he, too, had to leave the room.

"Reluctantly, he left the room. He later expressed to me a great deal of hurt from this confrontation. He couldn't understand why the blacks didn't trust and accept him as one of their own. After all, he had lived and worked among them for more than twenty years. He had believed that they did trust and had accepted him. Now, he's having his doubts."

Professor Sammy wanted to be sure the students understood what was happening. Walking up and down the aisles, he crossed the front and back of the classroom. He attempted to explain, "This incident brings out something that could be of great importance to us. Here's a white man who actually identified with blacks, only to find out in a time of crisis that he wasn't welcome within their midst."

"Can we ever really identify with another race or person?" Brenda asked.

"Identify with, or as? That may be the major dividing line no one can cross. Are you getting this?" He spoke at the top of his voice.

Janet joined the discussion. "Professor, what about over-identifying with one's own race? Isn't this also possible?"

"Are we more a race than human beings?" Professor Sammy quickly responded. Then added, "Maybe a black person thinks more intently about being a black person than a human being. Could this help perpetuate the view that the white race has of them—black beings rather than human beings?"

Allen wondered, "Perhaps we're over-identifying with color. We're not thinking 'human being,' but whether we're black or white. The white man does the same thing. It's the white man who focuses on color."

"Precisely," emphasized Professor Sammy, with his right hand jolting up and out.

"Yes," Mark added, "and that may very well be the biggest problem."

Alice was agitated. "With this mentality, I don't see how we can ever reach each other or ever live together peacefully."

Professor Sammy returned to the front of the room. Looking around and making eye contact with many of the students, he dropped his hands to his sides and calmly said, "Yes, of course we're going to be aware of our differences, but we'll be even more aware of them if we over-identify with color or race. The differences are obvious and naturally can't be totally ignored. However, they should be accepted, not worn as a label. Isn't this the reason that you're in this classroom?

"Let me remind each of you that you're here to learn to cross bridges, not to build them. If you wish to build bridges, become an engineer, not a counselor. The counselor must learn to cross bridges that have already been built—built from doubt, distrust, rejection, and every kind of negative material that man can think. Cross them. That's your work."

One young student ended the discussion with: "Then we'll be able to work toward a better understanding, not just for ourselves, but for this nation and the world."

The class consensus was that they all needed to think of themselves and others more as human beings than a particular color or race. Class was dismissed.

Carla was physically and emotionally moved by Professor Sammy and the students this morning. She realized how much more they gave to her than she could ever give to them. At one time, she believed that she was doing them a favor by just being here. This morning she knew who was on the receiving end. Just when she thought that her mind and heart had been stretched to their limits, new boundaries were dissolved.

Stan eyed her curiously. He knew immediately that something was bothering her. "Carla, what is it? What's wrong? Please tell me, let's talk about it. I want to help."

Carla wanted to tell him. She had planned to tell him and yet, she staggered. She was alarmingly pale, staring ahead absently. Stan followed the direction of her gaze. After a period of time, she walked over to where he sat on the sofa, stood beside him, and began with the most direct approach.

"Stan, the doctor found a lump in my breast. It's possible that I may have cancer and will need a mastectomy." Heaving a long deep sigh of relief, Carla gulped for air as though she'd been holding her breath for the past two days.

His dark lashes slowly gave cover and for a long moment he sat with his eyes closed. He opened them and reached for Carla's hand, and drew her down to sit beside him. Wrapping his muscular arms around her, he tenderly rocked her in a slow motion.

Carla buried her face in his chest, and soft sobs escaped. "Shhh, shhh," Stan said in a hushed whisper, as he gently stroked her hair.

Her head and heart were spinning. She loved Stan more than ever. She wanted him. "Make love to me, Stan," she whispered. "Tonight, now, while I'm still a whole woman."

"Carla, you'll always be a whole woman to me. Breast or no breast, you're a complete woman." Taking her chin with his hand, he tilted her head up and softly kissed her lips.

"You know how much I want you, but we both agreed to wait until we're married. This doesn't change anything. I love you more, sweetheart, not less."

She passionately needed to believe him and the firmness in his voice convinced her that he meant what he was saying. She admired his high-mindedness. She needed his love and support to help her get through the next two months. Losing him would have been unbearable. And never getting to see the baby again would have caused extreme anguish.

Stan decided, "We'll marry sooner than we had originally planned. Everything will be all right. You'll see. We'll have a home and perhaps some day a child of our own."

"I want that, too, with all my heart. I want to mother your sweet little girl. Stan, in my mind and heart, she is a child of 'our own.' She's already my little girl. I couldn't love her anymore than if I'd given birth to her."

Carla agreed to marry Stan in secret as soon as possible. Stan prepared to leave. "Get some rest, I'll take care of everything, don't worry. This has to be very tiring for you." He kissed her good night.

Stan was strong, sure in what he wanted. Southern chivalry, very much alive, rose to the occasion. He would protect her from the inner demons of doubt. With his warmth and reassurance, he left her with hope, hope for the future she had felt slipping away.

Sliding a nightgown over her bare body, Carla felt assured it was all right. They had risen above body parts. Pushing back the bed covers, she lowered her body, allowing it to experience the coolness of the sheets.

A long, deep sigh escaped her lips and Carla contemplated about the past month. The most tumultuous in her life. Riots. Three students killed. Many others wounded. Surrounded by violence. Surgery pending. A marriage planned. Change in ideas. Thank God the month of February had finally ended.

Yes, her ideas about blacks had changed completely. Blacks were individual human beings with all the same feelings, ambitions and abilities as whites. Most of all, their needs and desires were no different from any other human being. Segregation was wrong and harmful to both races.

She had made a complete turnabout. She had become color-indifferent—neither focusing on nor caring about a person's color or race. It was as though she had a brain transplant. When she looked in the mirror, she saw a person who looked like her, but who no longer thought like her.

When did she change? When did it happen? Was it when she was forced to walk on the grass? Was it that Saturday morning when the students made her feel so special, or that cold Saturday morning just a few weeks ago when she stood on the landing looking out over the campus? Did the gentle breeze that stirred the small piece of white paper stir this white heart? Had that gentle breeze changed a lifetime of bigotry?

She felt in mourning that cold Saturday morning. Perhaps it was for the person who had arrived on campus last summer.

Drifting off, sleep replaced contemplation.

18

Storm Warnings

Candlelight flickered a warm glow, as shadows flitted in a small stained glassed church in Orangeburg. Shadows would dominate the coming events.

Friday evening, the first weekend of March, Stan and Carla were secretly married. Her parents were made aware of her plans. They had wanted Carla to wait until she had finished school and had her health problems resolved. Two friends from Charleston attended. One was Mary T, against her better judgment. Mary T had done her best to warn Carla this wasn't a well-thought-out decision.

"For God's sake, Carla, the man is a bigot."

"No, Mary T, he's a segregationist."

"And you believe there's a difference?"

"Yes, I have changed. He can too."

Her parents and Mary T had failed and for the moment, all Carla's troubles were forgotten: the lump in her breast, the racial conflicts in Orangeburg, finishing the semester. She was married to a wonderful man who she believed loved her and had the courage to withstand family pressure.

Stan had planned a two-day honeymoon combined with business meetings. The business meetings enabled Stan to get away from his family without suspicion.

As the newlyweds drove away from Orangeburg, they were naively mesmerized by their consecrated love, which both believed would bind them for the rest of their lives. At that moment, it was what each of them wanted.

It was a difficult time for Stan. He wanted nothing more than to be with his bride. He felt like a sleepwalker surrounded by stilted events of no relevancy. The most agreeable exhilaration occurred when the meetings ended and he swiftly moved to where she was awaiting his return. *They finally had more time together, alone.*

In the evening, they decided to go out to dinner and to a movie. Stan chose the restaurant. He insisted that Carla choose the motion picture. Carla chose the movie, *Guess Who's Coming to Dinner?*

Watching the movie, Stan squirmed. He was irritated and could hardly wait for it to end. Driving back to the motel, Stan didn't hold back his opinion of the movie. His usual guarded self-control unraveled. The movie clearly had triggered something deep within him. His voice took on a hard edge.

"That movie was disgusting. We'll never allow anything like that to happen here." He was so adamant, so resolute.

Carla cringed inwardly and replied, "Stan, it was about a racial issue we are daily faced with, one that must be resolved."

"Nonsense. It's a plot by the communists to destroy this country."

Carla enjoyed the movie, which she believed was about everything she now believed in. The controversial film portrayed an on-screen romance between a black man and a white woman, and their determination to be married over the strong objections of both sets of parents. Carla's choice of film could hardly have been worse.

Why would she have even thought about selecting such a movie for them to see? Where were her brains? Having no good answers, she tried to justify her stupidity by thinking that because Stan accepted her attendance at State College, he would accept her belief in the equality of the races and the positive effects of integration. That being so, exposure to the idea of racial harmony through a motion picture would have pushed Stan a little in her direction.

Stan continued his barrage of insults. "It was a sickening display of moral deprivation. How disgusting can the movie makers get?"

The intensity of Stan's reaction astonished Carla. He didn't find it at all informative, interesting or entertaining. Carla wanted to believe that perhaps Stan just needed more time to get adjusted to the idea of having a wife who believed in integration.

Surely, Carla thought, this wasn't the time or place to unduly engage him in a racial discussion. This was to be a happy time between them. They would never recapture these lost moments.

Arriving back at the motel, Carla was disturbed by Stan's continuing outburst. The enmity had by now reached ridiculous proportions. His anger threatened her hope of ever developing a better racial understanding between them.

Even now, Carla wanted to believe when Stan met and got to know her black friends in Orangeburg, he was bound to like them. His views would change. He would, at least, tolerate integration. Carla had to hold on to that thought.

It took the better part of the evening for Stan to restore a semblance of calmness and adapt a conciliatory tone. However, that evening something had penetrated the well-constructed wall they had built around themselves—a wall that wouldn't allow anything, or anyone, to spoil what they had together. The realities around them had the power to encroach on their protected space. The relationship once thought indestructible was remarkably fragile. The honeymoon ended with ominous storm warnings.

Back in Orangeburg, Carla returned to the apartment and Stan to his home and family. Stan would continue to visit her as often as possible. The marriage would remain a secret until Carla finished the semester. Carla prepared herself for cold empty nights without his warm nearness. What cheered her was the fact that the semester was on its short end.

Carla continued to work a few hours a week at the State Employment Office. The staff persisted in being barely polite. They cared for her even less since the riots and killing of the three students. Their attitude toward the students mirrored the rest of Orangeburg.

On one occasion, she was at the office to help train a new counselor, young, part-time minister. Sitting with Carla in a private office, he commented, "I'm amazed at how well you work with blacks. How do you get them to open up to you like they do? I have to dig everything out of them. It's a real effort."

Carla attempted to share with him a little of what Professor Sammy was teaching her in class. She explained, "When you're working with minorities, you can give them all the information, testing, counseling and referrals you want, but that isn't going to really help them. Your main task is to help them overcome their fear of trying, their fear of rejection, their fear of being less than another human being. That happens when the individual knows you care whether he makes it, when he can feel that caring in his very bones." The young minister tilted his head slightly to one side and looked doubtful. But she still had his attention. She proceeded, "Dare to care. That's what I'm being taught at the college. Dare to care and dare to feel. Feel a caring in a place that permeates your entire being. Feel until those who you want to reach are touched by it."

He nodded. Her heart skipped a beat. If only a little bit of this was getting through, it was a lot.

"Professor Sammy says, 'Don't worry about being subjective. Caring, inner caring, isn't an emotional high that'll cause you to lose your objectivity. It's more like a soft wool blanket that gives another individual a warm, comfortable feeling. Even though an outer space remains between the counselor and client, the caring silently fills that space and creates a greater self-esteem within the client.'"

Hoping that her courage to dare to share was contagious, she poured enthusiasm into her statements. "My professor comes right up to us," she continued, "and looks intently into our eyes and tells us, 'Where others fail to reach the difficult, withdrawn individuals, the counselor who dares to care not only reaches them, but helps to lift them. Go ahead,' he concludes, 'be who you really are, a warm, caring, human being. Because if you're not that first, you'll never be a very good counselor.'"

The training session ended and the young minister thanked her. He seemed a little overwhelmed. Carla was hoping some of it did rub off. She was grateful for the opportunity to have shared a small part of Professor Sammy's teachings. She felt fortunate to have him as a teacher. This time, color didn't cross her mind.

That evening, in the statistics' class, the students were discussing the results of poll takers. Professor Santa Claus chuckled and reminded them, "Statistics don't lie." With a broad smile, he added, "but liars do use statistics. Statistics are used and abused. Be suspicious whenever you read statistics or hear them recited as proof in an argument."

"How do I tell valid statistics from those that are being falsely presented?" asked a student.

"Ask yourself how and why the research was carried out. What was the study's purpose? Who conducted the project that produced the statistics? What was their particular axe to grind? Never take statistics at face value."

Terry laughingly asked, "Is that true of people too?" Everyone burst into laughter. It was good to hear laughter in the classroom again. It had been a long time since they were this relaxed.

Who would have ever believed that statistics could be fun? It remained a difficult subject for Carla, but at least she didn't dread it anymore. The right teacher made the difference.

The following day, Stan and the baby came by the apartment. Their time together was overshadowed by Stan's fear that his family would learn they were married. His manly stature seemed to be shrinking in the space of a few weeks.

An agitated Stan informed her, "I'm trying to keep my older daughters from becoming too upset. They still miss their mother. I'm sorry, Carla, but my mother continues to hope that I'll break it off with you." Stan's remorse seemed sincere, and Carla could only hope time was all that was needed.

"Do whatever you believe is best for all of us. Perhaps with a little time and less pressure, your family will come to accept me." It was all she could say. She didn't wish to push him any further away from her. She still had school and work to keep her busy.

And there was always Professor Symbolic. In this Saturday morning's class, he was giving a report on the peaceful protest march by the students who had gone by bus to Columbia.

"I was out there marching around with the students. We all felt the tremendous amount of tension. We were forewarned there were machine guns all around us. There were officers up on the roofs and we could hear ourselves being intercepted by walkie-talkies that the officers were carrying. We all felt as if we breathed wrong, we would be in big trouble. The students, without exception, conducted themselves well."

Carla was proud of them. It was good to hear they all made it back without any kind of incident. The national news media reported the students had actually turned away from their own more militant leaders. The militant leaders wanted the students to charge the police lines. It took courage to walk away, but they did.

Carla was pleased to have the march behind them. Just six weeks of the spring semester remained to be completed.

Although the weather had gone from cold to pleasantly cool, Carla feared her relationship with Stan was going in the opposite climatic direction.

The light in Stan's eyes wasn't as bright these days. He had a lot to deal with at home. The family pressure to break them up was a constant irritant. In such a racially charged atmosphere, Carla's concern was that Stan's family's dislike for blacks would translate into a more deeply rooted resentment toward her. It was a predicament that caused dread to flood her veins.

At the moment, Stan was holding up, but the wear and tear showed in the newly creased frown across his forehead. His irresistible smile was less frequent and his beautiful blue eyes had taken on a troubled look. At times, there were long dark silences between them.

Carla was willing to overlook the harsh reality that was gradually creeping into their intimacies. She hypnotically clung to a reminisce of vows earlier spoken in a small church in Orangeburg. It was so wonderful to give herself to the man she loved—mentally, physically and spiritually. She gave freely and completely.

She had never realized she could, in such a short time, become so completely one with Stan as to lose consciousness of ever having lived without him. Yesterday was gone forever with its loneliness and today was filled with their love for each other.

When Stan was holding her or when they were making love, she was completely engrossed in their love. Concerns of cancer or his family's objections became irrelevant details pushed into the background and ignored or forgotten in a moment of bliss. At that moment, she was happy. And indeed, it was enough.

19

It Isn't Fair!

"I believe that the white man will learn to love the black man before the black man learns to hate the white man," said Professor Polite in class.

"It's an interesting and thought-provoking statement and it has quite a few implications. However, with all that has gone on in the past few weeks, how true can this possibly be?" mused a student aloud.

Professor Polite walked to where the student was seated, lowered his eyes and warmly addressed his concerns. "The black man continues to love. With all that has transpired between the races, he continues to want to love the white man. It's the white man who must learn to love the black man, and I believe he'll do so before it's too late." He returned to the center of the room.

James commented, "Perhaps this is what will keep the races from totally annihilating each other, the fact, or at least the possibility, that one race continues to love the other, no matter what."

Class was dismissed. But part of Professor Polite's statement pricked Carla. ". . . before it's too late." Coming from a gentle man as Professor Polite, the statement was quite disturbing. Wouldn't hate-on-hate wipe everyone out? Isn't that what James was really saying?

As Carla stepped outside of the classroom, Norton approached. His broad shoulders drooping, he appeared tense and reflective. But he was glad to see her. "Carla, you're still here?"

"Sure," she said in a matter-of-fact tone. Then, smiling, "Remember, I said I would finish the school year." They began to walk together.

"I had to miss last week and I wondered how you were coping." His interest was sincere.

"The best I can, Norton, but the past few weeks have been unsettling, to say the least." She was thinking of all that had transpired in her personal life as well as school.

Norton paused and stopped walking. Carla turned to look up at him. A broad mischievous grin, ear to ear, crossed his large black face. "Carla, I don't know if this is any comfort to you, but you'd make one hellava good Negro."

That got a big smile from Carla, but still she asked, "Why's that, Norton?"

"You have the fire. We blacks have a burning fire within and that's what keeps us going generation after generation. It stirs us, guides us, lights the way.

"Your Kennedy talked about passing the torch to each new generation. We don't need to pass it on. We come into this world with it burning brightly within us. Carla, you have some of that fire."

The sincerity and intensity of his words went right to the heart and Carla was deeply moved. She was more than comforted, she was honored. She probably had been paid the highest compliment that a black person could pay a white person. A year ago, she would've been insulted, repelled by the thought, but tonight she was proud.

Norton gently touched her arm, said good night, and took the steps down to his car for the drive back to Charleston. She was left with the warmth of his fire.

Touched by Norton's praise, Carla realized that blacks were a complete family—brothers and sisters all. They were looking from the inside out within their close family community, and we, the whites, were the outsiders. Did they realize this?

Carla found herself envying them. She marveled at the reversal of her fortunes. A year ago they were less, she was more. Now, they were more, she was less. They had so much more inner strength, so much more tolerance. Norton called it fire. She called it soul power.

Carla took the steps down to the street level where other students lingered. They were discussing the lecture. All were stirred by the professor's comments. But, then, he always had a way of doing that.

Brenda, James and Arnie talked quietly at the bottom of the stairs. Leaning against the banister, Carla quietly remarked, "The professor looks tired."

"We're all feeling a little tired," said Arnie. "The stress is really beginning to get to me. I can feel it."

"It's the longest semester I've ever lived through," Brenda added.

"And it's not over yet," James agreed. "Let's just try to get through it and stay cool."

"Good advice, coming from the class clown," Brenda laughed.

Saying good night, Carla started toward her car.

Arnie's voice followed her, "Where's your car, Carla?"

"Just a few feet away within sight," she replied.

She could hear them rising from the steps to keep watch over her. As Carla drove away, the kindness and care they expressed for her welfare went with her.

On the first day of spring, a bright sunny day, the many rich colored azaleas painted the campus and a plush carpet of green meandered beside the pathways. Carla visited with the dean. He motioned her to have a seat. Carla sat in her usual chair in front of his desk. "How's your class work coming along?" His voice was more somber then she had heard before.

"My classes are going well," she assured him.

"Dean," Carla asked, "has there ever been a white student to graduate from South Carolina State?" The thought had been on her mind of late.

He relaxed in his large chair, and said crisply, "None yet." His eyebrows rose. Looking at her with a tender smile, he said, "You'll be the first white woman to receive a degree in the history of the college. I don't expect any publicity, as far as the college goes."

"No, neither do I," she agreed.

"How do you feel about being the first?" His hands rose and gently rested on the desk.

A frown creased Carla's forehead. "I never thought about myself making history."

"You aren't just making it, Carla, you're living it. Eventually, someone will record it, but you'll have lived it. That's no small thing. And, you're accomplishing it under the most trying conditions."

"But you know, dean, it's nothing like I had planned."

He sighed. "It never is."

Carla left the dean's office with the assurance that her course credits were all in order and that, by the semester's end, she would have completed the necessary work for her degree.

Stan, and the baby spent Sundays with Carla whenever possible. She called Carla "mommy." It came natural for her. And it all seemed so right—the three of them being together as family.

Carla moved with ease from her white world to the black world. In Professor Santa Claus's class one evening, he was discussing the Black Power group. Compared to Professor Polite, his attitude was pessimistic, an interesting contrast and not at all like Professor Santa Claus.

"They're still threatening the black community and threatening to overthrow the white power system in Orangeburg—to burn the town down, if necessary. The militants haven't given up their goal in the least bit. We're now merely in a waiting period that allows them time to reorganize and to strengthen their ranks."

"Sir, what do you think they'll do next?" one student asked.

With a hollow voice, he said, "We're sitting on the edge of a volcano, waiting for it to erupt. There's no predicting what's next, and there's no preparing for it."

The students listen attentively. His seriousness caught them off guard. He summed it up, "The smoldering anger has ignited into a blazing fire—a fire that's out of control. When it's again brought under control, what will our lives be like? We're all wondering about this—and it's something for you to think about."

Carla thought about it. Blacks had been denied for so long that even if they got what was rightfully theirs, it still wouldn't guarantee the love and respect that Professor Polite talked about the other night.

The end of March was only a few days, leaving the students with just four and a half weeks of school. The campus remained calm. Although the threat of cancer intermittently plagued Carla, she managed to make all of the assignment deadlines, attend all her classes, and work part-time at the employment office. She also visited once a week with her friend Darlene at her home.

She continued to meet once a week in the school library with the study group. What had happened on and off campus drew them closer together. They didn't talk about it, but they were determined not to allow anyone or anything to undermine what they had together. In their own subtle way, the black students in the group looked after Carla.

It gave Carla the reassuring feeling that she was okay in their world. Regardless of the seemingly complex scheme of things, she trusted them, and although she was not one of them, she was one with them.

Leaving Professor Symbolic's class one morning, Carla was walking along the landing toward the steps when the professor called her back. She could only mutter, "Oh, oh, what now?"

The anxious moment caused her heart to flip as she stepped back into the classroom. Professor Symbolic walked toward her. With an unusually pleasant expression, he said, "Carla, I just want you to know the counseling tape you left with me two weeks ago is very good." His usual curt tone softened as he added, "I'm quite pleased with it."

This was the first time good old Professor Symbolic had paid her a compliment of any kind. Taken-a-back, she gushed, "Thank you, professor."

For a brief moment, their eyes met and they felt good about each other. He could go on with his "whitey" remarks and she could go on being a whitey. It was all right. For a fleeting moment, at least, they had touched that place of mutual respect.

Carla was reminded that this must be what Professor Sammy meant when he talked about crossing bridges. It was a great way to end the month of March.

April showers arrived, temporarily washing away the stain campus pain. The warm sunshine that followed bathed the campus in a new light, lifted their hearts, and gave hope for brighter times.

For the first time, the dean was late for a meeting with Carla. Sitting in the leather chair beside her, he looked tired, worn and distressed. Turning toward her, he apologized for the lateness and, in a low-keyed voice said, "Carla, these are difficult times for everyone, students and faculty. Family members of the faculty are also feeling the pressure."

Carla grimaced and said, "Yes, sir, I hadn't considered that they would also be caught up in the turmoil."

Sighing, he looked off into space. His eyes took on a glassy gaze. With a pensive voice, he intoned, "February is a month none of us will ever forget." He spoke aloud, but almost to himself.

"Yes, sir. I know I'll never forget it." The raw memory threaten tears to flood her dark eyes.

"It's been a long semester for us all," he wearily added.

"Yes, I agree. And it's not over."

The dean turned his gaze back to her. His face softened as he smiled and asked, "How could April possibly be any worse?"

Leaving the dean's office with a pervasive sadness, Carla felt a loss and deadly emptiness. There could be no returning to a simpler time. The dean's pain was obvious. He had a deeper understanding of the realities that the upheaval brought. He doubted a tranquil state would exist on the campus, or in the nation, any time soon.

The following evening, Carla attended Professor Sammy's class. So charged with high voltage that he electrified the entire class and gave her a much-needed lift. The students sat on the edge of their seats, eyes and ears alerted to absorb every possible morsel that his body language expressed in words and movement.

As his feet traveled up and down the aisle between the seats, he held them to the moment. As his hands would rise and fall, he taught as much with facial grimaces and hand movements as he did with every in-depth emphasis he released in words.

"Don't just learn counseling methods, techniques and theories from your teachers and textbooks," he implored. "Your clients will be your best teachers. Be aware that they bring you a gift every time they enter your counseling space. It's the most precious gift of all, the gift of themselves. Be sure to handle this gift with the utmost care."

Crossing the front of the room, he hesitated for a thoughtful second, turned his head quickly, and made direct eye contact with a student. "Anyone," he said, "can rattle off learned information about almost anything, or interpret test scores. You, however can be gentle and kind. Become aware of your client's every response. Listen for what they say, how they say it and for what they don't say. What they don't say often speaks louder than any sound that may tap the eardrums."

The silence settled in and not one of them stirred. He walked to the window, briefly gazed out and then suddenly turned about to face them. "Did you know that if you're tense, uptight for any reason, you send out a loud and clear message to your client? One that reads, 'There's no one here for you today. All doors are closed to you.'

"Please, please, get beyond the appearances of your clients. Don't expect the 'norm' from individuals who may have had to live with a lot less than the 'norm.' Don't turn away, because they may not be as clean as you would like or dressed according to your standards. Don't judge them from the place you're in at any given moment."

Professor Sammy put his right hand over his heart and spoke in a hushed voice, "Accept your clients wherever they may be in their moment. Be there for them by giving them your undivided attention. You can't do this if you're judging and condemning."

Class was dismissed. Leaving the classroom in hushed stillness, no one wanted to come out of the electrifying state he had put them. They knew not only was he teaching them but, he was giving them the responsibility for the teaching that he shared with them. He had shared his being with them. Keep the teaching alive, keeps him alive. It was a grave responsibility they all took serious.

What a teacher! Carla thought. He was so dynamic, so in touch, sooo—black. But where and from whom else could she learn so much about relating to and communicating with minorities, human beings? He didn't just teach—he was "a teaching." His class alone was worth her being here.

They knew now what the month of April could possibly inflict upon the students at State College and the nation. Infected with the darkness of hell manipulated by a national force of an awesome tragedy, the campus was again in mourning.

On 3 April 1968, the dean's rhetorical question was answered. Dr. Martin Luther King Jr. was dead, murdered by a cowardly assassin. The students at South Carolina State were in a state of disbelief and despair. Flood of tears and denials were everywhere. The fragile calm was shattered. The students didn't know to whom or where to turn with their pain, and neither did Carla.

The campus had become one large funeral parlor. Everywhere Carla looked, students were grieving. A quiet sadness enveloped their motionless forms. When a student joined a group, there was no greeting, just a meshing of intense grief.

Walking across the tear-stained campus, Carla barely could contain her own tears. Everyone, herself included, moved in slow motion. It was as though, without warning, a switch had been flipped. So deep and weighty was the grief that nothing and no one could move but a small distance at any given moment. No one wanted to move or be disturbed from the place they were in. They were all held captive by grief. There seemed no way beyond it.

Carla entered the library. Across the room, near the large front windows, sat a young male student, alone on the couch, divorced from his books lying on a low wooden table. His head was bowed, eyes lowered, arms resting at his sides. His hands were dropped, open in a defeated, lifeless gesture upon the seat cushions.

Walking over to him, Carla gently sat on the couch beside him. She softly placed her hand upon his open palm. They sat in abject silence.

Finally, slowly, he raised his head and turned slightly toward her gaze. Those large black eyes, usually full of light and mischief, were flooded with tears. He tried to speak, but could not. Carla wanted to say something, but could only whisper his name, "James, James."

He swallowed hard. "Carla, it's all over. His face streaked with tears, his voice was barely audible. "We've lost our Man. He was taken from us. He was our light, our possibility. It all seems so hopeless. No one can replace him. No one." He dropped his chin to his chest.

In the silence, Carla shared his pain. Abruptly he looked up as a spark ignited his memory and asked, "Are you going to class tonight?"

"Yes. Yes, I am." Carla quietly responded.

"Would you take notes for me? I'm just not up to going. Nothing seems worthwhile. They got Smitty. Wasn't that enough? School seems so useless."

"Sure, I'll take notes for you. But James, please remember what Martin Luther King Jr. lived and died for isn't dead. True, he can't be replaced, but you and others can keep his light shining brightly and continue what he started." Gently squeezing his hand she added, "James, education will be one of the most valuable tools to accomplish his dream."

Carla withdrew her hand, got up and walked toward the library door. As she reached the door, she heard, "Carla, Carla."

Turning around, she saw a determined James who stood and spoke. "Don't bother about taking notes for me. I'll be in class tonight. Thanks."

She tearfully smiled in acceptance, turned, and opened the library door. She took a deep breath, as though the fresh spring air would somehow relieve her heartache. Crystal and a couple of students stood at the bottom of the steps. "Hi, Carla. Using the library?" Crystal was solemnly distracted in her grief.

"Hello, Crystal. No, just visiting with James." Carla slowly descended the steps.

"I guess you heard what happened," Crystal said in a distressed voice.

"Yes, Crystal, I've heard." Carla spoke barely above a whisper.

Crystal squinted, wrinkled her cheeks and shook her head. "It's hard for us to believe. We keep saying to each other: Is it true? Did it really happen?"

"I know," Carla replied.

"Carla, you can never know or understand how deep this cuts. We just can't pick up and go with business as usual. The movement has come to a halt. Damn! It isn't *fair*! It's less than fair!"

"Crystal, I'm sorry."

Crystal's inner anger was momentarily unleashed. "What've you got to be sorry about? Your white world is still intact."

Crystal immediately took control, heard what she was saying, and was apologetic. "Ah, damn! Now I'm sorry, Carla. You don't deserve that. We're all hurting really bad right now. You can't have any idea how much. Please, don't pay me any mind."

"No apology necessary. I'll see you in class."

Walking back to her car, the deep and heavy sigh Carla heard was her own. Her heart felt what her mind could never express. There was no question but that this could only fester the raw memory wounds of racial quarreling and bitterness.

Contorted with agony, she opened the car door wide, hit the seat with her full weight, and closed the door. It felt good to be in the confinement of her car. Backing up, then going forward, Carla crept off the campus grounds, away from the atmosphere of a gigantic wake.

As she drove to her apartment, what Crystal said resonated. Crystal was right. Carla had no idea the hurt that was being felt by her classmates. She remembered when President Kennedy was assassinated. He, too, couldn't be replaced. However, the system, her white world, went on. It hadn't depended on one individual. Carla's possibilities had remained intact.

Now, Crystal, James, all of them believed that their dream of possibilities wouldn't be realized because it depended on one individual, Dr. Martin Luther King Jr. And that individual had cruelly been taken from them.

The depth of their grief had taken them to a place where uninvited forces would prey its wicked rage until all were in imminent danger.

20

An Inconsolable Loss

"He was larger than life itself for the students here and for the blacks all across this nation. Dr. Martin Luther King Jr. became our voice, our strength and our heart. He was able to get in touch with the black soul-identity and our sense of well-being, restoring our belief in ourselves. All of this has been abruptly and violently disturbed."

Professor Polite attempted to console the class. In unison, the students whispered a tearful, "yesss."

"We will survive!" The professor spoke in a strong, convincing voice. "Yes, for a time our loss is inconsolable, and I suspect there's a hurt that will never completely heal."

Not a dry eye could be found in the classroom. Plunged into an abject misery, intermittent low distraught moans mingled with the professor's eulogy.

"This nation is immersed in violence. Racial violence is widespread in many states. A violence that has resulted in the loss of a great leader. Dr. King wasn't just a black leader, he was an extraordinary leader of men and ideals—ideals that were rooted in a love for all of mankind. This is the legacy he has left us all, black and white.

"We have the responsibility to nourish these lofty ideals and to bring them to full fruition. There's a tremendous amount of work for us all to do. More now than we could've ever imagined.

"Grieve. But don't get lost in your grief. Dr. King would want and even expect us to continue what he had just begun."

One student sobbed, "This will change history."

"History is constantly being changed by either great men or fools. The great men lead and the fools use guns. Either way, history is changed," the professor sharply replied.

The professor dismissed the class. The students exited in a state of hushed, tearful silence. Carla slowly left the classroom caught up in the professor's statement, "The responsibility would be theirs for the rest of their lives."

Noticing she was deeply affected, Norton approached. "Carla, we shall overcome this too."

"But, Norton, is the movement really badly hurt?"

"It's hurt really bad, but we shall go forward. You know, Carla, Dr. King gave us the 'present.' I could get up in the morning and actually believe that equality and justice could exist now—not tomorrow, but right here and now."

Norton stood straight, tall and proud. "We were always in the moment, a glorious moment. And that's the major difference. We'll continue to work now for a better tomorrow. The movement has lost its present. But it will always have its tomorrow."

"Norton, can you, can blacks wait for tomorrow?"

"Before this happened, I would've said, 'No, hell no!' But now the very bone marrow of shock restrains us. We haven't come to a full stop, but we're moving at a slower pace."

Norton gently placed his hand on Carla's shoulder. "Carla, you best be careful. A lot of angry individuals are on and off campus. White has never been their favorite color, and now it's a gross insult. Don't take any chances."

They parted and Carla was left with the belief that with men like Norton, the movement would move forward at a brisk pace. She needed to believe that. It helped to ease the hurt she was feeling.

That evening, Stan visited. He couldn't understand why Carla should be adversely affected by the death of Dr. King. She wanted to share with him her feelings of loss. But she couldn't explain it to him. He merely shrugged off the incident. Stan was relieved, almost jubilant in his belief that things would once more be as they were—separate and unequal.

He reassured her, "The local black community will quiet down since they've lost their national leader. Their troops are scattered and there's an internal struggle going on within the black power groups. It's a struggle that'll destroy the black movement's integration progress." This didn't comfort her. Carla's heart flushed with despair.

But he didn't come to discuss Dr. King's death. He had dismissed that easily. He came to possess what was his and there wasn't much time to lose. He must be home with the family soon. His recent visits were hurried and increasingly less affectionate.

On Friday afternoon, 5 April , at 5:00 P.M., South Carolina State and Claflin College students walked to the Memorial Plaza in Orangeburg and knelt for three minutes in silent prayer.

The assassination shattered any hope for any improvement of the relationship between the students and the city of Orangeburg. The school's campus became a breeding ground for the black militant groups.

Talk of retaliation was heard from the more militant students. A feeling of helplessness pervaded. Emotional ambiguity had everyone living out of fear. No one was sure in which direction the anxiety-ridden grief impelled the student body.

As the students' anger grew to monumental proportions, in the hope of preventing violence, undergraduates were ordered home early for Easter break. Wanting to know whether the order included the evening graduate student class, Carla stopped by the dean's office.

Pleased to see her, the dean informed Carla, "Tonight's graduate class will be held. Because of the spontaneous decision, the graduate students would have no way of knowing about it.

"During a trustees' meeting, there was a question-and-answer period," he explained, "most of the questions were being asked by members of the black militant group. Things got out of hand during the discussion about the new auditorium."

So much sadness was in his voice. "The militants want the new auditorium named for the three young black students who were killed in February during the riots. However, it had already been decided that the auditorium will be named for the individual who made the auditorium possible by acquiring a bond. So, we had already decided to name the auditorium in his honor.

"A new men's dormitory is in the planning stage, and we agreed to place a plaque with the three names in front of it. The militants told us to go to hell."

Tilting back in his chair behind his desk, the dean raised and lowered his arms in a gesture of total resignation. "Carla, you can see that this type of unreasonableness is very difficult to cope with. I can't deal with this kind of anger and senseless behavior. The discussion became so tense that the president of the college felt the students could be in imminent danger. So, he announced that the Easter break starts immediately after lunch today."

"I'll be going to Charleston for the Easter break, right after class tonight. I can use a break right about now," she informed the dean. Carla left his office wishing that she could help, but there was nothing she could've done or said to ease his pain.

Because their marriage was still a secret, Stan would spend Easter with his children, mother and former in-laws. Carla was wretched that she wasn't included in Stan's family life. On the drive to Charleston, she feared family pressure was starting to get to him. Stan made no attempt to hide from her the effects his family was having on him. The more sharp critical attitude, anxious gaze, and the sad mouth were more frequently confronting her.

It was a lonely holiday without Stan and the baby. With the Easter break about to end, Carla found herself not wanting to go back to classes. The past weeks had taken their toll and perhaps her personal concerns and the riots in other cities were beginning to get to her. She was weary of the disturbance in both her inner and outer life.

Dr. King knew and understood that the greater force existed through nonviolence, the persistent public acts of nonviolence. The movement had taken a menacing twist, and without his steady hand and voice of calm, it could take a more violent turn.

And there was Mary T to contend with. Mary T always believed that this wasn't a marriage made in heaven. She saw the deepening sorrow manifesting itself in Carla. It hadn't been easy for her to stand back and watch Carla drowning in an illusory love. With a warm mother's aching heart, she admonished Carla. "I don't like the way Stan handles or mishandles the situation with his family."

"But Mary T, it's such a difficult situation for him." Carla did her best to defend him.

"Carla, he lacks the courage to face up to his responsibility toward you."

"Please just be a little more patient with him. In time, they'll come around." Carla wasn't sure that she believed her own words.

Once back at school with her friends, Carla was relieved that there hadn't been any incidents during the break. Stan hurried by for a short visit. Conversation was strained and their lovemaking drifted into a routine sexual performance.

Darlene and Carla had become genuine friends and they made the conscious effort it took to deepen a friendship. Today was her first visit with her since Dr. King's assassination. Normally, they talked about school, their lives, their families, and didn't dwell on issues of race. This time, it was different. Carla sat at the table in the kitchen. It was, in many ways, like her visits with Mary T.

Darlene had set a pretty china cup and saucer with a red flower pattern before her, and said, "Carla, I've been concerned about how all of the violence these past weeks is affecting you." Darlene put the kettle of water on the stove.

"Well, I've had my ups and downs, not only with this violence, but some with personal problems. But this hostility..."

"This hostility needs to be dealt with," interrupted Darlene, "but you have to understand, it's always with us. Racial conflict is swept under a rug or out the back door."

The whistling teapot told Darlene it was ready. She brought it to the table and poured the tea into their waiting cups. Hot steam rose from the cups, reaching toward the ceiling. She joined Carla at the table, and they sipped their tea. Darlene thoughtfully replaced her tea cup upon its saucer and continued, "I believe that hostility must be addressed. The riots, three deaths, and now Dr. King's killing, are too much racial turmoil to shove aside or sweep under anything."

Darlene's voice never altered, nor did she appear angry. She remained matter-of-fact, pleasant, and calm. "It's strange," Carla reflected aloud, "before attending State College, I was completely oblivious to racial strife."

"Of course you were. Most white people can't understand why blacks shouldn't be satisfied with less—less education, less pay, less decent housing, less self-esteem, less dignity. I think it comes from wanting to believe that we're less human. It makes it more comfortable for them"

Carla's own situation with Stan came immediately to mind. "I think you're right on target about the comfort part. Having to face up to being so wrong for so long not only rocks the boat, it overturns it."

Darlene's slender brown fingers gently touched the rim of her teacup. "It surely does, Carla, and the water is just as cold and polluted as their prejudices."

"And so easy to drown in," Carla added.

"How are you and Stan getting along?" Darlene hadn't met Stan, and didn't know that they were married. She was aware there was a relationship between them and that there were racial issues to be resolved.

Carla cast her eyes downward and said, "Stan has me worried."

"It's not going well, is it?" Darlene was quick to pick up the implication.

"No, Darlene, I just can't reach him. His attitude toward the college hasn't changed."

"Of course, it hasn't. Why would it?" Darlene's eyes searched Carla's in surprise that she expected such a change.

"Well, I've changed, and I was hoping Stan would at least become a little more tolerant." She sighed and sipped her tea.

"Carla, you're not understanding the difference," Darlene said in an almost exasperated voice.

"What difference?" Carla curiously questioned.

Darlene obliged in no uncertain terms. "You exposed your emotions—perhaps not intentionally—but you did just the same. And that's when the heart opens, love steps in. Change is the natural result. You let your guard down. It'll never happen with him. Stan will never allow that to happen to his heart. He'll stand guard and protect his emotions from ever being exposed to blacks."

"But, Darlene, he's a good man," Carla pleaded. "He just hasn't associated with blacks. He hasn't had the opportunity to know them."

"Yes, you're right and he'll make sure the opportunity never presents itself. Carla, you're fighting a losing battle with that one." Her voice softened, You love him, don't you?"

"Yes, I love him," she mournfully admitted.

"Well, Carla, it will be a rough and bumpy road with him. I hate to see you subject yourself to that kind of abuse. But I can see you're not about to give up on him. Defeat of any kind is a difficult experience. But, Carla, knowing when to give up is a form of accomplishment also."

"Yes, you're right." How like Mary T she was!

Their friendship deepened with their agreed conclusion cementing a feeling of oneness.

Leaving Darlene's house, Carla experienced the first good feelings she had since 4 April. Darlene was a wonderful friend. It was good to be able to share with her. Carla wished she could've shared with her that she was married to Stan. But this wasn't the time for any new revelations.

Three weeks after the King shooting, the campus seemed again to be on a positive track. No disturbances occurred and Carla's relationships with classmates and professors were friendly and relaxed. It was a relief not having to keep her guard up.

However, most of the white community of Orangeburg hadn't changed. It remained a segregated community with extreme prejudices toward blacks. They seemed to be hopelessly locked into an ignorance intensified by a mask of fear.

Most of Carla's time was spent on campus. With just two weeks of school left, James and Carla met in the school library. They reviewed the semester's class materials to prepare for the long-dreaded comprehensive and for the oral and written review of the school year.

Their worlds had changed since they first made plans to study together for the almighty comps. World events came and went, but the plight of a graduate student was ever the same. If they didn't pass both sections of the comp test, they didn't earn their degrees.

Sitting on the couch where she had comforted him just a few weeks earlier, Carla sorted through a year's worth of test results. James sat on a cushioned chair directly across from her. They placed their books and stacks of papers on the low wooden table between them and began the arduous task of preparing each other. Soon, their papers covered the entire length of the table, spilling over onto the floor.

After hours of reviewing the materials and drilling each other, they agreed to call it a day. Exhausted, they gathered up their papers now in chaotic disarray, and stacked them on top of their books.

James sighed wearily. The old mischievousness was gone. This difficult semester had taken its toll. It had taken from him a close personal friend and a dear national one.

"It's been a long two years for me. This past semester has been the longest yet. I'm glad it's coming to an end."

"It's been a strange semester, to say the least, but you've handled it well," Carla complimented him.

"Yes, Carla, it shouldn't have taken such a great loss for me to grasp what my own father tried so hard to impress upon me."

Bending slightly forward, Carla touched his hand. "James, you're no different from most young people who believe that education and fun go together. The problem is blacks have a lot of catching up to do, and your father is much more aware of it."

Looking somber, James said, "My father knows the degradation of being black and not having an education. You can bet it won't happen to his son!"

"No, James, I don't believe it will."

They picked up their materials and left the library. James walked Carla to her car and said, "Goodnight." Carla watched him walk away and thought, there goes an outstanding future teacher. If any good did come out of these tragic days, it was James' awareness of the value of a good education.

Carla's relationship with Stan continued its downward slide. He continued to live with his three children in a small community outside the city of Orangeburg. The town was a white Baptist segregated community, determined to stay that way.

Spending quiet time together, Stan ventilated, "Since the day I told my family about your attending State College, there has been nothing but turbulence. They're becoming more vocal every day. In their minds, you might as well be a nigger."

"Stan, that's a pretty strong indictment coming from them. It has to hurt you."

"Carla, we always have been staunch segregationists, but I believed once you were finished with that school, my family would accept you. I still hope they will."

Carla dared not even to ask Stan what happened if they continued to refuse to accept who she was. She wasn't prepared to hear the answer. Stan and the baby had become an integral part of her life. She had to believe that it would work out.

The month of April started with an inconsolable loss of a national black leader. The end of it threatened another painful loss—a personal one.

21

Paying the Price

"Hey, Janice, let's have lunch while we're downtown."

"Sure, it'll be great getting away from the school cafeteria for a change," she replied. They both laughed as Carla pulled into a parking space in front of a local restaurant.

Turning the ignition off, opening the door part way, Carla sensed a hesitation from her passenger. A sorrowful silence hung in the air. Leaning back on the car seat for a long, anguished moment, they glanced through the large glass window of the restaurant. Seeing only white patrons in the restaurant jolted them back to the existence of two different, separate worlds. Carla had given Janice, a student from one of her classes, a ride downtown.

They were on their way back to campus. It was lunch time. Why not eat downtown? For a naive split second, they both had forgotten there would be a problem.

Again, Carla reached for the door handle, swung the door wide and said, "Let's go have lunch."

Eyes lowered, in a hushed voice Janice whispered, "Carla, they won't serve me."

"But we're together," Carla protested, "they can't refuse."

She looked at Janice and saw the hurt, the pain. Carla closed the car door, turned the key in the ignition, backed away and headed for the school cafeteria. At school, they had the freedom to share lunch, and, hopefully, to laugh again.

Out to enjoy the day together, they both had forgotten the differences people could perceive between them. It was a rare moment. If only they could've cast the shadow of forgetfulness over the entire nation, what a blessing it would've been.

Carla learned a valuable lesson that afternoon. When another individual was denied, it infringed on Carla's own rights. Janice's denied right had taken away a right from Carla—the right to go where and with whom, she pleased. Racial prejudice didn't just touch Janice, it reached out with its long sticky fingers and touched Carla.

It hurt, made her feel dirty, both angry and withdrawn. She wanted to strike back, but felt helpless. Carla experienced only the least of the symptoms that Janice had endured on a daily basis.

That evening, Carla found herself having dinner with Stan at the same restaurant she had driven away from earlier in the day. Its all-white patrons reinforced the day's earlier lesson.

Stan slumped in his chair, frowned, picked at his food and was uncharacteristically impatient with the waitress. Carla felt they needed to talk to get what was bothering him off his chest. She knew very well what the subject of the conversation would involve. She didn't want a foolish squabble to come between them, but she couldn't see any way of avoiding it.

"Stan, do you want to talk about what has you upset?" Carla cautiously asked.

"Carla, my family and friends are buzzing with the news that we plan to marry." Stan was agitated. He moved nervously in his seat.

Carla stiffened and tactfully suggested, "Stan, perhaps you should tell your family we're married. It would put an end to the gossip mill."

"I had hoped to soften the hostility before telling them. But everyone is up in arms at the very thought of it. It's just unthinkable to them that I would marry you." Stan momentarily looked away from her. "In fact, they warn me that to marry you would be to risk my good name." Stan was intensely serious. His blue eyes were pierced with the fear of discovery.

Carla found that ironic. She thought her name was pretty good too. But, ah, this gave her some idea of just how small-minded these people were, and the depth of prejudice she was up against.

"Their minds are like concrete," she jokingly responded, trying to lighten the mood, "all mixed up and permanently set."

Stan didn't appreciate the humor. Their evening ended at the apartment. Stan took her to bed, but he was clearly preoccupied over the wrath of his family and friends.

Lying in bed long after Stan had said goodnight, Carla shivered at the thought of the damage that little minds were capable of doing. Was it possible they could threaten what she and Stan had? Could they possibly destroy a marriage that had barely begun?

With one day left in the semester, Carla visited the dean. As she entered his office, the dean's pleasant smile returned. "Well, Carla, I'm sure we're both pleased that this difficult and emotional school year is finally coming to an end."

"Yes, I am. I also want to thank you, dean, for all the help you've given me the entire year, and especially for caring."

"Carla, it's the least I can do."

She hesitated, and then added, "You know, dean, I'm not accepted in the local white community anymore."

Exasperated, he shook his head, "Yes, you have a lot to live down."

"No, dean," she defiantly said, "I have a lot to live up to."

His shoulders dropped, he sat back, arms and hands, fingers entwined, rested on his lap, and thoughtfully he said, "You know, South Carolina State may have prepared you for one of the greatest challenges of your life. You may be asked to prove your human worth within your own white community."

"You may be right, but I'm not ashamed of having attended South Carolina State.

"All right, Carla. I know you have the inner strength to deal with adversity. I witnessed that strength many times over the past year." The dean got up from his chair extended his hand and Carla rose to accept his warm handshake.

As Carla approached the door, he said, "Please remember, commencement services. I'll expect to see you then."

After seeing the dean, Carla stopped by Darlene's. Over tea, Darlene talked with Carla about a recent experience she and her husband had in Columbia. "We were in a shoe store. The owners were so friendly. Not just polite because we were customers, but genuinely warm. They cared about us as people. We struck up a conversation with them and came to find that they were from Orangeburg. Who would expect whites from Orangeburg to be so nice? We're guilty of racism too when we judge all whites in Orangeburg for the actions of a few individuals."

"I guess it's human nature to accuse others of the very thing we do ourselves," Carla injected.

"After that experience, I won't be able to make blanket judgments about anybody," Darlene agreed. They smiled, sipped their tea, and realized they could always learn when they allowed themselves the freedom to talk with each other.

Carla's year at South Carolina State was complete. She had received an excellent academic education and had learned far more about human and racial relations. Her education had encompassed mind, heart and soul.

The night before her departure for Charleston, Stan visited and they reviewed their plans. Carla was to immediately check into the hospital for the breast biopsy.

Stan reassured her, "As soon as you're able to travel, I'll come for you."

The light was gone from his sky-blue eyes and his beautiful dark lashes seemed a little duller. He promised, "I'll bring you back and we'll live in my house with my girls. My family won't like it, but they'll get use to it."

Stan walked to the large picture window and gazed into the darkness. In a quiet distant voice, he said, "I'll tell them we're married soon. I promise."

Stan struggled with the decision he continued to avoid. The time was fast approaching. He must tell his family about their marriage. It could be a matter of only a few days. Still, he was in the grips of panic at the thought of facing them with the truth.

The courage he had shown beside Carla at the family dinner had long dissipated. He was left with promises that he wasn't sure he could keep.

Carla glimpsed the indecisiveness in his voice. "It's all right, Stan, I can be patient with them. We can tell them together when you bring me back," she said.

Stan slowly turned away from the window as if Carla's voice called him back from a distant place. He sat on the sofa next to her. Gently touching her face, he ran his hands through her hair. Then, moving his hands to the back of her neck, he drew her to him. He covered her mouth with his and kissed her hard. His weight moved her backward onto the full length of the sofa. Slowly and methodically, he removed her clothing, her undergarments. All the while, kissing her face, neck, shoulders, and cupping her breast, sucking the nipples until they responded to his demands.

His touch became heavy. He dove into her with a force bordering on anger. He couldn't devour her quickly enough. He strived to take her mind, body and soul. He wanted all of her and he wanted it now.

Never had she known him to be so forceful, so demanding. But with a heart intoxicated with desire for him and a body on fire, she withheld nothing.

Lying awake long after Stan's apologetic goodbye, Carla felt his presence. Closing her eyes, she fell asleep to his almost tearful promise, "Carla, I promise we'll be together soon, for the rest of our lives."

The following morning, a clear, sunny May day greeted her. It was her birthday. Taking a long, deep breath, she approached her car for the drive to Charleston. A hospital bed awaited her arrival.

With Mary T by her side, Carla checked into the hospital. Hours later, she felt a firm pat on her cheek. A distant voice repeated, "Good news, Carla. Good news. Wake up, now. Everything's all right. It's good news."

Through blurred vision, slowly reentering consciousness, Carla made out a white cap and uniform. Then blinking, hard, it hit her. The biopsy was negative. She didn't have breast cancer.

She was whole, she happily repeated to herself. "I'm whole! I'm whole!" Yes, it was good news. Flushed with sleep, she drifted off with but one thought, Stan. Stan would be coming soon.

Three days later, at Mary T's house, Carla waited for her husband's arrival. Sitting together on the couch, Mary T insisted for the umpteenth time, "He should've been with you. Just phoning to see how you are is a very poor form of support." Mary T's steel blue-green eyes were livid.

It was Mary T who was there for her at the hospital. Mary T who stood by her bedside, comforting her, keeping her spirits up. Mary T who walked with her through the darkness of the unknown.

"It's all right. He's coming now. Everything will be all right. You'll see," Carla assured her.

Mary T was finding it difficult to forgive Stan for the way he had treated Carla. Furious, she reminded Carla, "He can't even stand up to his own former in-laws or his mother. He'll always put them first. You'll be hurt every step of the way."

"He just needs time to allow them to become adjusted to the idea of our getting married. We'll tell them together tomorrow," Carla pleaded.

"You don't believe that any more than I do," Mary T said with a smirk. "Carla, all eternity will not be enough time. They'll never accept you as a human being, much less a wife. The difficulty is your inability to acknowledge it."

"My mind hears what you're saying, Mary T, but my heart has no ears. I just have to keep trying to reach them."

Carla wanted her caring friend to understand she and Stan were caught up in a whirlwind of events that had taken over their personal lives. Carla wanted to sit out the storm, in the belief it would pass, leaving them unscathed.

Mary T leaned toward Carla and took her hand. Her voice softened, "Honey, you'll never be able to bend far enough. You will break. As stubborn and persistent as you are, you will still break."

A knock on the door announced Stan's arrival. Mary T offered Stan a pleasant surface greeting, beneath which beat a mother's heart that would kill if necessary to protect her chick. They left immediately for a nearby motel. In the morning they would return to pick up Carla's personal belongings. Mary T wouldn't be home, but Carla had a key.

Stan was quiet, distant. He told Carla he was tired, that it had been a long day. Carla readily accepted his explanation. Tomorrow would be a difficult day for both of them. They would face his family together as husband and wife. They would tell them the truth and, once they knew, Carla reasoned, she would be accepted and the dark clouds hovering over their lives would slowly dissipate. The stress and tension between them were to be expected. They prepared for bed, made dispassionate love and fell asleep.

Early next morning they returned to Mary T's house. Carla unlocked the door and she motioned with her hand toward the couch, "Stan, have a seat in the living room while I get a few things from the bedroom. I won't be long." Carla cheerily called out to him from the bedroom. "We can pick up the books later." Silence. "Everything we're taking today is already packed." A troubled silence.

Coming back cautiously into the living room, Carla saw a visibly shaken Stan. "Stan? Is something wrong, sweetheart?" Rushing to his side, she sat next to him on the couch, took his hand and asked, "Stan, sweetheart, what's wrong?"

Head slightly bowed, eyes in a trance like stare, he spoke barely above a whisper, "Carla, I can't do it. I can't take you home to live with my girls. I told them that we're married, and what our plans are."

Carla's life was obliterated before her eyes. Distinctly pale, tongue momentarily paralyzed, she looked at him with troubled brow. "What?" was all that could slip past her lips.

"My mother and in-laws are in shock. They can't believe I could do something like that to them. My older girls threatened to leave the house if I bring you into our home. Everyone identifies you with the niggers at State College. To them, you're a nigger."

Numbed, she wasn't sure exactly what it all meant. A long silence expressed its presence. Finally, her voice found, she asked, "Are you saying that you want more time?"

He stood up and faced her with pressed lips, tightened jaw, and determinedly said, "No, Carla, I'm saying it isn't going to work."

"Stan," she pleaded, "What about us? What about the baby? We've become so very close. Am I to give you and her up?"

Slightly lowering his head, his strong jaw tightened. Looking directly into her eyes, he said, "Carla, I'm even more concerned for the baby. I don't want my child around niggers, playing with niggers. I would never allow it."

Still laboring in disbelief, Carla gulped down the threatening sobs, she questioned, "Are you saying I could never visit a black family or take the baby with me to their home?" In a swift moment of clarity, she saw it coming now. The storm headed directly for them, it would make a direct hit. She couldn't get out of its path. They couldn't get out of its path.

Shadows trampled on his face as the twisted look of racial hatred claimed its victim. Gritting his teeth and clenching his fists, Stan spoke from rage and fear. "That's right! I don't want any niggers near my child. Carla, my family was right. I can't compromise my beliefs. I'm a committed segregationist." So, Mary T was right, what he was saying is he is a confirmed bigot. Stan continued, "I'll fight against integration in every way possible. If the public schools are integrated, I'll put my girls into private school. No matter how far they attempt to enforce integration, I'll always teach my children the evils of it."

"Stan," Carla tearfully injected, "what if the private schools integrate...what then?"

"My girls and my family..." he looked down toward Carla, chest expanded and proudly reaffirmed, "There's always a way around it. We'll always be committed segregationists."

Carla was beaten. Stan's voice took on a quieter tone, less intense, but firm. "Carla, you have to understand. I thought you were attending State College only because you counseled minorities. I expected that after you were finished there, you would separate it from your personal life. But Carla, you actually like them. That's what scares me. I could never allow my wife to have nigger friends, to go into their houses or to ever bring a nigger into my home."

"But Stan," with quivering lips, she softly pleaded, "you don't even know them. You could possibly…"

"Yes," he interrupted, "and I don't want to know them. A nigger is a nigger. You or anyone else is never going to change that."

"Stan," she begged, "isn't there any possible way that we can work out our differences? I would do almost anything to keep us together."

Stan, looked whipped, his usual twinkling blue eyes were dull, lifeless. He took a long deep breath. With a doubting sigh, he slowly said, "Carla, can you put the past year behind you and assure me and my family that you'll take a firm stand with us against integration?"

How could she explain to Stan that her relationship with blacks was indissoluble? It took a year immersed in a black environment, driven by an intense desire for a graduate degree that she thought she couldn't get any other way. It took a year of almost forced integration for her to begin to see things the way they really were, to drop the blinders of hate and fear. It took that gentle breeze to stir a white heart. It took walking on the grass.

She didn't change because she was being tolerated or treated equal but separate. She changed because she was denied the dignity of human recognition. She felt the alone, unwanted existence of being different, being nonexistent, a nonentity. She only recognized the truth of humanness after she was subjected to a hurt that no Band-Aid, however large, could cover.

Then came the awareness that a loving God wouldn't set out to degrade the very differences that it had created. It wouldn't deny to these human beings the choice of caring and sharing within these differences.

Carla's tearful silence told Stan all he needed to know. Stan walked to the door, opened it, and turned to face her. He softly whispered, "I'm sorry." He was gone.

She couldn't abandon her hard-won growth or sacrifice the greater good she had obtained. She wasn't about to live a lie when she so recently learned the truth. Her husband must either love her as she was or not love her at all. The choice was Stan's, and he made it.

Carla continued to sit, dizzy-headed and confused. Baffled by the unexpected occurrence, she asked, what had happened? How could she have been blind-sided? Weren't all the signs there? She tried her best to shake off the disbelief and despair.

With tears profusely streaming down her face, she sat in her own sorrow drowning. She had nowhere to take this god-awful pain. Carla sank into the depths of despair when she thought Stan couldn't take her home with him because his family and friends identified her with blacks and that for all practical purposes they considered her one of them. She sunk lower into these depths when she understood the prejudice and the hate directed at her black friends. She moved into the depths of hell's bottomless pit when she realized she would never see Stan or the baby again.

She cried aloud, "God, haven't I been tested to the limits, and now this? Will I break?"

22

Rhythm of Her Heart

Mary T returned and wasn't surprised at what had taken place. She had seen it coming. Mary T didn't say, "I told you so." She just tried to comfort Carla as best she could. Carla's heart had been on overload for the last year, and now her heart was breaking into a million pieces. There was no comfort.

After Stan walked out, Carla wanted to crawl away and die. Instead, she returned to work in the Charleston Youth Opportunity Center. She wasn't about to abandon the work she was just beginning to understand. She hoped that, if she threw herself into her work, she could dull the pain.

Carla expected to be welcomed at the agency with open arms, as a person with a unique perspective, as an individual who could make a valuable contribution to the office serving minorities. She was wrong. Given the job of answering the phones, she did no counseling.

Remonstrating, she was ordered to the main office in Charleston for a possible transfer there. Taken into a private office at the rear, Carla was introduced to the supervisor—a short, heavy-set, bald man in his late fifties.

Ordering her to sit, he began an angry interrogation. "Why would a white woman go to a nigger school? How could you spend that kind of time and closeness with a bunch of jungle bunnies? How dare you expect to work in my office!"

The dean's poignant words, "Carla, you will be a marked woman.... You may be asked to prove your human worth," resonated while the little man fervently announced, "Carla, we don't want anything to do with you and, if I have my way, no one else in Charleston will either. You're a disgrace, not fit to work with white people." His anger didn't mystify her. He was, after all, a confirmed bigot.

Standing up, facing his contempt, Carla very softly stated, "Fine. I also prefer not to work with you." Walking to the door, opening it and without looking back, she left behind his astonished gaze. She returned to her office and wrote her resignation. The very reason Carla had exposed her mind, heart and soul in a year long struggle no longer existed. Another chapter closed in her life. Giving up Stan meant giving up the baby as well. Graciously, Stan allowed Carla to visit with the baby for a final goodbye, after which she was to be taken to her grandmother.

Driving to her grandmother's house, Cathy was very talkative, a happy three-year-old who was immersed in the joy of having a new mommy.

"Will you take me for a train ride, mommy?" she asked excitedly.

Carla didn't know how to reply. The baby asked again and Carla responded, "I'm sure you'll ride a train someday, sweetheart."

"And can we go to the big pool and play? The one with the really big sandbox?" She was stretching her little arms wide to describe the sandbox.

"You mean the ocean with its beautiful beach like daddy and I took you to a few weeks ago?"

"Yes, mommy! That one!"

"You like the beach, don't you, baby?"

"Oh, yes. But do you know what I like most of all?"

"What, sweetheart?"

"I like having a daddy and a mommy."

All too soon they were approaching the grandmother's house. Carla parked in front of the house where the grandmother awaited their arrival.

Carla wanted to say so much to this beautiful child, but could not. She wanted to tell her, "I do love you as much as if you were my very own, my very own child to love, to care for and to help guide. I would protect you with my life. However, I can't protect you from the white world that you're living in with your father. A world where the heart posts a sign—'whites only.' I can't protect you from the racial bigots of this world.

"I want so very much for you to know I'm not rejecting you. I could never do that. The decision to give you up isn't one of choice. It's a dear price being paid for what I believe within my very soul."

But she was too young, too innocent to know or understand. Carla was tormented with a decision she would have to live with every moment for the rest of her life. Saying a final goodbye to this sweet, beautiful child was torturous.

As Carla was stopping the car, Cathy energetically waved to her grandmother. No longer was there time for words between them. As soon as the car was completely stopped, Cathy was out of the car, running to greet and hug her grandmother, who she dearly loved.

Stooping to embrace her with one last hug, Carla pressed her close and whispered, "Always remember that I love you, baby."

"But, mommy, aren't you staying with me?" She began to understand. Tears formed in her eyes.

Choking up with emotion, Carla could hardly speak above a whisper. "No, sweetheart, I must leave now. Be good and be happy."

Forcing the little arms from around her neck, Carla straightened up and quickly turned toward the car. Moving as fast as she could, she couldn't look back. If she did, she knew she wouldn't have the courage to drive away. Teary-eyed, she reached for the blurred car door handle.

"Come back soon, mommy. Come back soon."

Cathy was and always would be her little girl. Nothing could ever change that. That little child's cry and face would be in her heart and memory forever. Their encounter was brief, and yet it felt like an eternity.

Managing to start the car, Carla drove away—away from everything she ever wanted, a husband she loved and a beautiful child she adored.

The black community didn't ask her to do this. How could they understand her hurt any more than she could fully understand theirs? They both lacked the ability to understand the cost of each other's struggles. True, their price had been much greater, and they've been paying it for much longer. Carla was obeying an inner force greater than any she had ever known. The price to dissolve a marriage and give up a child seemed high, but she was paying the price.

Carla returned to South Carolina State for commencement day, a day of heartfelt farewells to her many friends. Here she was again, a lone white face in a sea of black. But color no longer mattered. Proud to be counted among them, she was free, without racial prejudice, a freedom to be herself. This was a beginning, not an end.

Sitting among them, she prayed, Lord, teach her to love those who would discriminate, enough to hurt others, into an awakened truth, a truth that would cut into the heart in order to pour love into it.

The College choir sang *The Impossible Dream*, the theme song for the rest of her life. Norton, Crystal, Darlene, James and others, all dear and precious friends, although they would go their separate ways, she wouldn't forget them. They would always be with her—the rhythm of her heart.

23

Postscript, 2001

Since that fateful year at South Carolina State College, in Orangeburg, South Carolina, I never saw Stan or Cathy again. In my heart, at least, Cathy never ceased being my little girl. My brief marriage to her father was annulled in Florida, where I had immediately moved and worked as a counseling supervisor, teaching young lay black men and women to counsel other blacks.

Mary T and I have kept in touch over the years. However, due to the constant moving and traveling, I lost contact with my student friends at State College. They, like Cathy, have remained part of who I am, my existence. The entire experience was indelibly imprinted. None of the individuals or events could ever be erased from my mind, heart or soul.

Although I never had children, I have been fortunate enough to experience the love of a true soul mate, a love without hatred toward any one. He was the blessing of my life.

Eventually, I was certified as a counseling psychologist. Over the years, I've been deeply involved in efforts to improve human conditions. In the beginning, working with black causes for equality led me to work with young Native Americans. I led and was a party to litigation that involved racial and gender equality in the work place that reached the United States Supreme Court. This effort saved fifteen thousand jobs.

Remember, when I finished telling the story, I said it was a beginning, not the end. The full implication of my traumatic transformation in 1968 was made clear to me in 1973...visiting a shrine in Lourdes, France. I had a transcendental experience that caused me to actively seek a spiritual path.

I traveled the world, studying with Hindu, Buddhist and Christian masters. These years and experiences were recorded in a diary and are written for publication entitled, *Walking With Mary and Jesus.*

I've learned through work and life experiences that racial problems have no quick fix. Working out these problems requires a conscious and constant vigil, similar to the on-guard stance that preserves our nation's freedom. Today our racial problems continue to fester.

I once emphasized to James the importance of education. I still believe that. However, I would also respectfully suggest how important it is that black and white Americans are educated in the classroom about society's inherit racial enrichment. In a diverse society, racial differences and similarities bring the possibility of greatness to its people as a whole. If the history of the black civil rights movement is taught to black *and* white students, the blacks' struggle for civil rights would be appreciated, respected and admired by both races. Education on social acceptance that's taught in schools and society will make the difference.

When we don't mutually respect differences and lack the ability to use these differences, to full advantage, society is doomed to an internal restless violence on our streets across the nation.

It is the open practice of personal values that influences others and shows a concern for racial equality. It's what the individuals within a society are willing to openly practice that will be the most influential.

As a new generation puts the lie to false myths, society has the arduous work of reconditioning what it has taught previous generations. This is the area in which we tend to fall short. It requires more time, effort and resources than most societies are willing to give. However, it remains the most productive step a diverse society can take if it is to assure a harmonious twenty-first century and beyond.

A young native American client once asked me, "Why do you care what happens to me?"

"You're a human being," was my immediate response.

Whatever is happening, we're in it together. Each human life affects all human life. The big picture is made up of small ones. In our human reality, there isn't a separate you and a separate me. There's an individual you and an individual me who are one in our humanity. It's our common ground that unites us one to another. It's what we live and breathe in.

A point blacks have long labored to get across to white America is that integration is an accomplishment, but recognition of their humanity as human beings is a necessity to their well-being. In the early sixties, black students didn't protest to just sit at lunch counters. "We are trying to eradicate the whole stigma of being inferior. We do not picket just because we want to eat.... We do picket to protest the lack of dignity and respect shown us as human beings."[9]

Individual acceptance of the humanity in each of us, regardless of race or color, is learned through empathy of differences and similarities, individual mutual respect, self-esteem and caring for each other, social love.

The definition of social love is the realization that the rights and privileges that we enjoy belong to everyone, every human being regardless of the racial, ethic, and religious heritage.

For those who continue to struggle to open their hearts to social love, the mistake may be in believing that the challenge must be accompanied by an act of bravery. Thus, there's a lack of recognition for the moment, and we continue our sleepwalk, waiting for a time of drama in our lives.

Through life's process, I've observed that each of us is asked at various moments, "Choose ye who ye shall serve." Unfortunately, many of us fail to hear and respond, or if we hear, we pretend we do not.

---

[9]Harvard Sitkoff, *The Struggle for Black Equality 1954 -1980* (New York: Hill and Wang, 1981) 86.

In actuality, the challenge is continuously arising, and the act may require something as easy and simple as making eye contact or allowing a gentle smile that reveals, "I like you and respect your humanity." The list is endless.

The opportunity to express social love is presented through many tender choices in each our lives simply and often. Any one of these opportunities could be my moment, your moment or our moment of social love.

Most of us want to believe that love would cure all of society's ills, but we look to others for the where, what and how of it. It's talked and written about as if it were a commodity, boxed or bottled, to be purchased from some mystical supermarket shelf. But caring love is a gift not to be found there, but rather from within each individual, where it sits waiting to be unwrapped.

Social love includes the expression of what we are as a people, culture, and nation. It flourishes when it's shared freely among its people. To be free from human prejudice, regardless of the circumstances of birth, is to open one's heart and find the gift of social love that lies within. Each of our hearts is ours to open or ours to close. The heart, after all, is the hand that touches the face of God.

For me, delicate lessons evolved out of the racial interaction, causing the realization that neither race had the slightest awareness of the struggle that was required for the other race to experience this awareness.

The benefits we offer each other far outweigh any selfish gain we could possibly contrive by going it alone. It does take courage, risk and service to stand up and to be counted, to overcome. But isn't this the stuff that love is made of?

In October 1995, I read, for the first time, the book *The Orangeburg Massacre*.[10] The authors meticulously researched and reported in-depth the events through which I had lived. I was stunned to learn how precarious my own life probably had been

---

[10]Jack Bass and Jack Nelson, *The Orangeburg Massacre* (Macon GA: Mecer University Press, 1984).

during those turbulent days. In the eye of the storm, guardian angels do exist, white and black.

The question which I'm asked most often is, "If you could choose one from all of the traumatic experiences you had at State College, which would you say was the most difficult or mind boggling?"

My answer is always, "Invisibility." Invisibility dissected my mind and spirit. I still cringe at the painful memory of those days of invisibility among the students. Other discrimination practices are harmful to one's self-esteem, but there is a basic need, in each of us, to know that I exist. I can only get that assurance from your respectful recognition of my humanity. You may not like my skin color, but, for God's sake, don't ignore my humanity, my existence as a human being. This I believe is the most diabolical racial practice that blacks have had to endure for generations.

The events that I experienced many years ago are not, unfortunately, dated. Racism in the Twenty-First Century hasn't moved much beyond the late sixties. With all of the medical, technological and industrial progress our nation has made, one area remains stagnant. This nation's last frontier to conquer isn't outer space. It is racism. Nineteen sixty-eight is yesterday and today; The challenge is not to make it tomorrow as well.

For many years, I have expended my efforts to bring about national recognition to the three young men who gave their lives for the civil rights cause. It is with this book that I sincerely hope the respect, dignity, and admiration for those young men may at long last be hailed.

So, the final question must then be asked, was it worth it? Yes, yes, a million times, yes. To be free from human prejudice, regardless of the circumstances of birth, is to open one's heart and find the love that lies within. Can there be a greater joy?

I once believed that I walked this path without choice. Today, I walk it willingly.

Dear reader, will you walk it with me?

Epilogue

The Investigation

Attorney General Ramsey Clark conducted an investigation of the Orangeburg Massacre. However, he found the evidence key to the investigation was compromised. The U.S. attorney in Columbia, would not cooperate. A grand jury refused to indict the police officers who killed the three students.

Clark charged the officers with depriving the students of their civil rights by killing them. A South Carolina federal court jury found them not guilty.

Clark remained convinced. "They committed murder. That's a harsh thing to say, but they did it. The police lost their self-control. We are lucky more weren't killed."[11]

In 1993, Frank Beacham, a New York-based writer, posited, "Looking back at the killings 25 years ago may give a lesson on police violence."[12] The 25th year of the incident was marked with an American Public Radio docudrama written and directed by Mr. Beacham.

In 1970, two journalists wrote a book, revised in 1984, called *The Orangeburg Massacre*,[13] which described the killings as a South Carolina cover-up.

---

[11]Frank Beacham, "Orangeburg, America's Forgotten, Tragedy" (Los Angeles CA: *Los Angeles Times*, 1993) 5 February.

[12]Ibid.

[13]Jack Bass and Jack Nelson, *The Orangeburg Massacre* (Macon GA: Mercer University Press, 1984).

Appendix

The following are additional radio announcements recorded by Carla immediately after the student killings from 9 February 1968 through 14 February 1968. This is a verbatim transcription, including the grammar and spelling.

"All classes at state college are canceled. The tool company has canceled the evening shift and would close tomorrow at the end of the 'A" shift. U.S. Plywood has also agreed to cancel work shifts. The Orangeburg high school basket ball game is canceled. The Southern Methodist Church and Southern Baptist College valentine party is cancelled.

"The city of Orangeburg came to a complete halt between 5:00 P.M. and 6:00 A.M. An eerie silence envelops the city. The streets are deserted except for the occasional person rushing home from work or a solitary car cautiously making its way to some destination, and then, only in broad daylight.

"Orangeburg is dutifully abiding by its curfew. The curfew has stopped all activity in Orangeburg, as of course it was intended, and there is nothing to report at the moment from the heart of Orangeburg.

"Watson [a prominent politician] was in Columbia for an appreciation dinner, and he said he wants the Orangeburg disorder looked into as part of the general riot investigation begun by the federal government last year. Watson used these words:

"'The constant cry of police brutality is one the communists have used for years. It should be obvious Stokely Carmichael, Rap

Brown and Cleveland Sellars and their cronies would capitalize on such an expression. I'm going to do my part to see that these anarchists are prosecuted to the fullest extent.'

"The twenty-five year old Seller, coordinator for the student non-violent coordination committee, was reported wounded in last night's rioting in which three negro students were killed and thirty-seven persons were wounded in gunfire between students and police. Sellers has been charged in the riots and is held under a 50,000 dollar bond.

"Watson said, Sellers is a native of Denmark, South Carolina, a community near orangeburg. He is reported to have made trips to Hanoi and Havana.

"Watson said, he would also like the investigating committee to include Martin Luther King in its continuing investigation.

"Watson said, King is trying to put a respectable mask on the face of black power, as he plans a mass civil rights demonstration in Washington in April. Governor Robert MacNair has accused advocates of Black Power of sparking the violence."

"About 600 National Guardsmen are in Orangeburg. Many of those sent to help the state highway patrol to seal off the virtually deserted campuses of the two negro colleges and to stand guard in the downtown business district. Others are standing by the armory.

"The Guardsmen have rifles and bayonets, as spokesmen at the armory in Orangeburg said, 'They are under order not to load their guns, but to keep their ammunition in their pockets unless their lives are threatened.'

"The state NAACP asked President Johnson to send National Guard troops from outside of South Carolina. It said those in the Orangeburg area are white-oriented.

"Biracial temporary Human Relation Committee met today with D.O. Pendarvous, members of the City Council, and other community leaders and officers of the U.S. Department of Justice's Community Relations Division.

"Fred Miller arrived from Atlanta to represent the Federal Government in the peace efforts. The Director of the South

Carolina Legislative Council, Henry Lake of Columbia, is in Orangeburg as a personal representative of Governor MacNair.

"Dr. McCloud Frampton is the chairman of the Human Relations Committee. He was asked whether the Committee had made any progress in today's secret meeting, which lasted a few hours. He said, 'It made tremendous progress,' but would not go into details.

"The Deputy commander of South Carolina National Guard Colonel, R.L. McCrady, called a news conference this afternoon. Colonel McCrady said, 'Before you is Major General Harold R. Barred, who is the Commanding General of the 51st operational headquarters in Columbia. He commands headquarters of the National Guard of our State, which basically has control of all of the National Guards in South Carolina.'

"Colonel McCrady informed newsmen there had only been a slight increase in National Guard's personnel during the past twenty-four hours. Some troops have been added to man the four armored personnel carriers which have arrived in Orangeburg.

"As for plans tonight, Colonel McCrady said, 'In anticipation of what may happen this evening, our basic plan of approach is almost identical to as we used last we evening, which I have discussed with you earlier this morning. We will undertake the responsibility of guarding numerous local utilities installations in the orangeburg area.

"We have personnel in and around the shopping area and the telephone exchange, with uniformed policemen patrolling the several school areas in Orangeburg.

"In addition, we will provide assistance to the law-enforcement agencies. Due to certain positions really I'm not able to disclose at this time, but generally it's in keeping with our efforts to try to assure students on the campus are maintained in their general positions, as was asked by the Governor in his proclamation.

"Newsmen asked Colonel McCrady, just what did the Governor mean by a state of emergency? He add, 'No marshal law was imposed as far as he was concerned. An emergency is securing something, situation where we have got a group of people who seemingly are intent upon causing a destruction to property, imposing violent acts on bodies of individuals. It is an emergency situation that has to be controlled.

"Chief of Police Roger Postens states his department will cause no undue hardship on citizens of Orangeburg in connection with the 5:00 P.M. curfew."[14]

With strained anguish in his voice, a minister read a statement issued by a group of nineteen ministers from both races in Orangeburg.

"We know that the world today is in a highly chaotic condition. All of us should be aware of the basic problems. These problems are international, national and local. Problems of poverty, civil rights, racial discrimination, world peace, morality. The problems of the world of college and university students on campus and off campus.

"These problems confront the people of Orangeburg: unrest and violence, hate, prejudice and even revolution will engulf us unless somehow we are willing to establish essential and effective lines of communication so that we may understand the needs and problems of one another. We must bear in mind that no individual, no home, no community will be safe until every home and every individual is safe, and that not one of us is as strong as all of us.

"Here in Orangeburg, we appeal to all of our citizens, all races, regardless of class, creed or color, to put away hatred and animosity and racial strife in a solid attempt to find peaceful and permanent solutions to our problems.

"We believe that every human being has a right to human dignity and the blessing of benefits of human existence, and a changing, and we hope, a developing world. This we believe can't be achieved unless we, as civic-minded and spiritually intelligent people of all races, sit and carefully direct in a tremendous effort to resolve our own difficulties without violence and bloodshed.

---

[14]C. R. Mancari, Taped Radio Announcement, Orangeburg SC, February, 1968.